THE OFFICIAL
Harry Potter™
COOKBOOK

WIZARDING
WORLD

THE OFFICIAL
Harry Potter
COOKBOOK

⚜ · BY · ⚜

Joanna Farrow

SCHOLASTIC INC.

WIZARDING
WORLD

CONTENTS

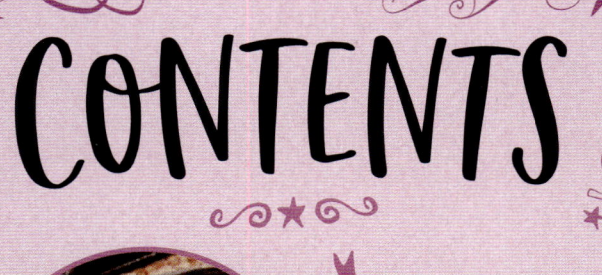

36

38

28

WIZARDING SKILL LEVEL

To help guide you, we've given each of our recipes a lightning bolt difficulty rating, from one (beginner) up to three (intermediate).

⚡ BEGINNER

⚡⚡ EASY

⚡⚡⚡ INTERMEDIATE

MEALS

16

50

26

52

82

62

60

CONTENTS

106

90

104

DESERTS & TREATS

88

86

100

DRINKS

DIETARY FLAGS

Following a vegetarian, vegan, or gluten-free diet? Look out for these colored flags, as they'll tell you which recipes are suitable for you.

 V Suitable for VEGETARIANS

 VG Suitable for VEGANS

 GF Suitable for those on a GLUTEN-FREE diet

If you are making a vegetarian or vegan recipe that requires food coloring, sprinkles, or other store-bought items, always make sure to check the manufacturer's ingredients and select a plant-based option.

WELCOME TO THE OFFICIAL HARRY POTTER COOKBOOK

40+ magical recipes inspired by the films of Harry Potter!

Wands at the ready, because you're about to go on a spellbinding kitchen adventure. Lots more than one, in fact! This official cookbook is bursting with delicious recipes for you to try your hand at, from "*Levicorpus*" Upside-Down Cake and Professor Sprout's Zingy-Springy Herbology Patch to Hagrid's Huge & Hearty Stew.

Each dish in this book is inspired by the films in the Harry Potter series. Whomping Willow Soup on pages 62–63, for example, has zucchini and cabbage tendrils that resemble the tree's violent branches, most memorably seen when they attacked Harry, Ron, and the Ford Anglia in *Harry Potter and the Chamber of Secrets*. Meanwhile, Grindylow Gulp, on pages 116–117, is a fruity drink with a water demon lurking at the bottom, just like the unpleasant little creatures in the second task in *Harry Potter and the Goblet of Fire*. (Don't worry, though, these Grindylows are made out of pear!)

Once you've selected the snack, meal, dessert, or drink you fancy creating, ensure that you have all the ingredients/utensils needed. (A list can be found on each recipe.) If you're following a vegetarian, vegan, or gluten-free diet, look out for the little colored flags as well, as these will tell you if the recipe is suitable for you. Another thing to keep your eyes peeled for is lightning bolt symbols. They signify the difficulty rating of each recipe, from one bolt (beginner) up to three bolts (intermediate). If you're still too young to apparate, always make sure you have an adult with you while cooking, especially when using something sharp or handling anything hot. Turn the page for more helpful kitchen safety tips.

Now, all that's left for you to do is channel Hermione's keen mind, Harry's famous bravery, and Ron's legendary love of food (especially this last one), and you're ready to get started.

Happy magical cooking!

KITCHEN SAFETY

Before you start cooking, read these 8 top tips for staying safe in the kitchen. They'll ensure that when you do begin, everything goes magically.

Tip #1

Wash your hands for at least 20 seconds with soap and hot water, then dry them thoroughly with a clean towel.

Tip #2

Put on an apron to protect your clothes, and if you have long hair, tie it back. Make sure you're wearing something on your feet too, just in case you break anything.

Tip #3

Read through the recipe in advance, making sure you have all the ingredients and utensils you need.

Tip #4

Keep the area where you'll be working nice and clean (and make sure it stays that way as much as you can as you go along). This will stop germs and bacteria from spreading.

Tip #5

Ask an adult to help you when using knives and machinery or working with hot ovens or pans.

Tip #6

Remember to always wear protective mitts when using the oven, and always chop away from yourself when using knives. (Turn the page for more simple knife tips.)

Tip #7

Never serve food when it's piping hot or only partway cooked.

Tip #8

No running or flying in the kitchen.

IMPORTANT!

On occasion, if not handled properly, food can make you unwell, so always wash fruit, vegetables, and herbs before using and keep raw meat and fish away from other foods.

If your chosen recipe does include raw meat or fish, use a separate cutting board, if possible. And make sure to wash your hands afterward.

Cooking Basics

The recipes in this book are designed to be easy to follow. But here's some extra info to make things even simpler.

~ ESSENTIAL TOOLS ~

Just as a potion needs the right ingredients, a recipe needs the right tools. Unlike powdered horn of a Bicorn, however, the following should be easy to get your hands on.

Liquid measuring cup

Scales

Tongs

Oven mitts

Dry measuring cups

Non-stick frying pan

Cutting board

Measuring spoons (used for both wet and dry ingredients)

Saucepan

Colander

Peeler

Baking dish

Prep bowls in lots of different sizes

Whisk

Wooden spoon (for stirring)

KiTCHEN SPEAK

Learn these, and you'll soon be talking like a proper chef!

BAKE: to cook food with dry heat (usually in the oven)

BEAT: to mix ingredients together quickly using a spoon, whisk, or blender

BOIL: to heat a liquid until you can see bubbles rising to the top

BROWN: to cook over high heat until food changes color

CHOP: to cut food into small pieces

DESEED: to take the seeds out

DICE: to cut food into small cubes

DRAIN: to remove liquid from food using a colander or strainer

DRIZZLE: to pour a liquid (such as a sauce) lightly over food

MARINATE: to soak food in liquid to tenderize and add flavor

PEEL: to remove the skin

PUREE: to mash, grind, or blend a food until it's completely smooth

SEASON: to add salt, pepper, or other seasonings to food

SIMMER: to cook a liquid just below boiling point

ZEST: to remove the outer layer of citrus fruit such as lemons

SiMPLE KNiFE SKiLLS

Lots of the recipes in this book require the use of a knife. If you're a young cook or just learning, here are some tips for doing this properly and safely.

1. Choose a knife that comfortably fits your hand.

2. Ask an adult to make sure the knife is sharp.

3. Always cut and chop on a wooden or plastic cutting board. (If the board starts to slip, place a wet tea towel under it.)

4. Hold the knife firmly by the handle with your strongest hand (usually the one you use for writing). As if you were holding a wand, in fact!

5. Make sure the sharp side of the blade is pointing down.

6. Use your other hand to hold the food, curling your fingers around the ingredient like a claw and then tucking your fingertips safely out of the way (no stray thumbs please!).

7. Cut downward with firm pressure, away from your body (keeping your eyes on the knife at all times).

8. Clean the knife immediately after use and store away safely for next time.

SNACKS

"Here, eat this. It will help!"

PROFESSOR LUPIN

These tasty and varied snacks will
keep you going when hunger strikes—be
that morning, noon, or night!

QUIDDITCH!OS

 SERVES 4 · ⏱ **10 MINS** · 🍳 **35 MINS**

A cheesy, meaty nachos recipe with a wizarding world twist—it's inspired by the game of Quidditch. Mixed in with the tortilla chips are Bludgers (meatballs), Quaffles (shrimp), and a single corn kernel (the Golden Snitch). Will you be the lucky one who gobbles up the Snitch? For added mealtime magic, follow our Top Tip at the bottom of this page to make Quidditch goalposts—they'll look amazing when you serve this.

10 oz/300 g beef or lamb meatballs

8 oz/225 g breaded shrimp/prawns

6 oz/180 g plain tortilla chips

1 corn kernel

1 cup/200 g hot or mild tomato salsa

1 bunch scallions/spring onions, chopped

4 tbsp finely chopped cilantro/ coriander

1½ cups/180 g grated cheddar cheese

Guacamole and sour cream, to serve

1 Preheat the oven to 400°F/200°C/gas mark 6. Scatter the meatballs in a roasting tin and bake for 10 minutes. Add the shrimp to the tin and bake for an additional 10–15 minutes or until both meatballs and shrimp are cooked through.

2 Scatter a third of the chips into a large shallow baking dish. Arrange half the meatballs, half the shrimp, and the single corn kernel over the chips. Spoon over half the salsa and sprinkle with half the scallions and cilantro. Sprinkle with half the cheese. Scatter with half the remaining chips. Arrange the remaining meatballs and shrimp on top and spoon over the remaining salsa, scallions, and cilantro. Add a final layer of chips and sprinkle with the rest of the cheese.

3 Bake in the oven for 10 minutes or until the cheese has melted. Serve with guacamole and sour cream.

Pipe cleaners

Cardboard and craft sticks

TOP TIP

Create your own simple Quidditch goalposts using cardboard and craft sticks or (if you want to make it really easy) pipe cleaners. Shape them as shown and, for added impact, you could even turn them gold with a food-safe paint.

Paint them gold

TOP TIP

⚜ ★ ⚜

Don't give the game away and
let anyone see where you
position the single corn
kernel in the dish!

HOGWARTS TRUNK OF FOODIE FUN

🍽️ SERVES 2　　⏰ 1 HOUR　　📅 15 MINS

With its house ghosts, ever-changing staircases, and portraits of famous witches and wizards who are always on the move, Hogwarts is a truly magical place. But one of the things the students who go there love best is the scrumptious food. This recipe shows you how to make a trunkful of Hogwarts-inspired treats, including a book of spells; a quill; pumpkin, Sorting Hat, and cat-shaped sandwiches; a tomato Remembrall; and Sirius's two-way mirror.

1 egg yolk

2 tsp water

Natural brown food coloring

9 oz/250 g puff pastry

2 cheddar cheese slices

¼ cup/40 g milk chocolate chips, or chopped chocolate

1 scallion/spring onion

2 small tomatoes

Butter for spreading

4 slices brown or white bread

Soft spreadable cheese, for sandwich filling

2 clementines or tangerines

2 small sprigs celery leaves

Tube of silver decorator frosting/icing

SPECIAL EQUIPMENT
Shaped cookie cutters
Fine paintbrush
Pastry brush

1 Preheat the oven to 425°F/220°C/gas mark 7. Use paper to trace and cut out the quill template (see page 120). Line a baking sheet with parchment paper. Beat the egg yolk in a small bowl with 2 tsp water. Transfer a little to a separate bowl and beat in a dash of brown food coloring.

2 Roll out a third of the pastry on a lightly floured surface to ⅛ inch/3 mm thickness. Place the template over the pastry and cut out the quill shape using a small kitchen knife. Transfer to the baking sheet and cut out a second shape. Use the knife to make small cuts all the way up both sides of the quills. Roll out the remaining pastry to the same thickness and cut in half. Place the cheese slices on one half and sandwich with the second. Cut out two 3½ x 2¾ inch/9 x 7 cm rectangles. Add to the baking sheet.

3 Use a pastry brush to brush the tops of the pastries with the uncolored beaten egg. Use the colored egg to paint the markings on the quills as shown in the photograph. Bake for 8 minutes until the quills are golden. Remove the quills from the pan and bake the rectangles for an additional 5 minutes.

4 Melt the chocolate using the process explained in the Top Tip. Scrape out onto a sheet of parchment paper and spread thinly. Chill until firm.

Continues on page 20

TOP TIP

To melt chocolate, place the chocolate chips in a heatproof bowl and rest it over a small pan of simmering water until melted. Alternatively, microwave on medium power, in short spurts, stirring frequently until smooth.

Quills

Book of Spells

5 Cut two long thin strips from the scallion, each no more than ¼ inch/5 mm in width. Place in a small heatproof bowl and pour over a little boiling water. Leave for 2 minutes, then drain. Wrap a strip around each of the tomatoes, tying the ends to secure in place.

6 Butter the bread and sandwich with the soft spreadable cheese. Cut out shapes by pressing firmly with your cookie cutters.

7 Push a small hole into the top of each clementine or tangerine and insert a celery sprig into each.

8 Snap the chocolate into irregular shards to resemble the two-way mirror. Pipe a zigzag line of decorator frosting onto the chocolate.

9 Trim off any ragged edges from the cheese rectangles. Using a fine paintbrush and brown food coloring, paint "Book of Spells" onto the pastry.

Book of Spells

TOP TIP

Pumpkin, cat, and hat cutter shapes work perfectly for this recipe, but you can use whatever you have on hand.

McGonagall (in her Animagus cat form)

Sorting Hat

Pumpkin

MAGICAL FACT

Along with their acceptance letter, first year students at Hogwarts receive a list of books and equipment they'll need for the coming school year. A trunk is perfect for storing all their school supplies—as long as they can get it onto the train!

MR. WEASLEY'S FLYING FORD ANGLIA

 MAKES 10 **45 MINS, PLUS COOLING** **15-20 MINS**

During their time at Hogwarts, Harry and Ron have countless hair-raising adventures, like the time they fly Mr. Weasley's enchanted Ford Anglia to Hogwarts and crash into a very unamused Whomping Willow tree. Ouch and ouch again! You definitely won't need an Invisibility Booster to make these car-shaped cheesy treats disappear. Serve them as part of a party spread or just on their own.

1½ cups/190 g all-purpose/plain flour

¾ stick/85 g butter, diced

1 tsp mild chili powder

½ cup/60 g finely grated Parmesan cheese

1 large egg yolk

1 tbsp cold water

TO DECORATE

4 tbsp softened cream cheese

Several radishes

Handful of red grapes

SPECIAL EQUIPMENT

10 wooden Popsicle sticks/ice lolly sticks

Small plastic piping bag

Food processor

1 Preheat the oven to 375°F/190°C/gas mark 5. Line two baking sheets with parchment paper. Trace and cut out the car template on page 120.

2 Put the flour, butter, and chili powder in a food processor and blend until the mixture resembles bread crumbs. Add the Parmesan, egg yolk, and 1 tbsp cold water and mix until the ingredients form a dough.

3 Turn the dough out onto a lightly floured surface and, using a rolling pin, roll out to a scant ¼ inch/5 mm thickness. Place the template over the pastry and cut out the car shape using a small sharp knife. Transfer to the baking sheet and cut out as many more cars as you can from the pastry. (You can also re-roll the trimmings to make more.)

Continues on page 24

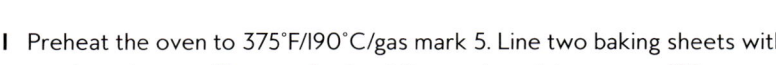

TOP TIP Make sure you ask an adult to help you when cutting out your car-shaped pastry.

Place a halved lemon or pumpkin on a plate or board (cut side facedown). Make cuts through the fruit with a small sharp knife. Carefully push the ends of the Popsicle sticks into the fruit so the cars are supported in an upright position.

4 Carefully push a Popsicle stick up through the base of each piece of dough, pushing the dough down onto the stick to secure it in place. Keep the Popsicle sticks as horizontal as you can when positioning them so you don't tear the dough. Bake for 15–20 minutes until pale golden. Leave to cool on the paper.

5 Spoon the cream cheese into a small plastic piping bag and snip off the tip so the cheese can be piped in a thin line. Use to pipe lines onto the crackers for windows, doors, and headlights. Use very thin slices of radish and grapes for the wheels, securing them in place with small blobs of cheese.

MAGICAL FACT

Sixteen different Ford Anglias were used during the making of the Harry Potter movies, each one adapted differently depending on its intended use. For shots inside the car, some were even cut entirely in half!

CHEESY PARSELMOUTH PASTRIES

    MAKES 10 · 40 MINS · 30 MINS

In the wizarding world, a Parselmouth is a wizard or witch who can talk to snakes. Harry discovers that he has this "gift" when he inadvertently helps a boa constrictor escape from the zoo, and then later overhears the Basilisk's murderous mutterings. Yikes! You'll learn a new skill of your own when making these tasssssssty mini serpents. "Choux pastry" uses a soft, piping paste that puffs up as it bakes and is so yummy to eat.

FOR THE PASTRY

½ cup/65 g all-purpose/plain flour, plus 1 tbsp

½ stick/55 g unsalted butter

2/3 cup/150 ml water

2 large eggs

½ cup/60 g finely grated mature cheddar

1 green pepper

TO FINISH

½ red pepper

Several raisins/currants

SPECIAL EQUIPMENT

Large plastic piping bag

½ inch/1 cm plain piping tube

1 Preheat the oven to 400°F/200°C/gas mark 6. Line a large baking sheet with parchment paper. Sift all the flour onto a square of parchment paper.

2 Put the butter in a saucepan with ⅔ cup/150 ml water and heat gently until the butter has melted. Bring to a boil and tip in the flour from the parchment paper. Remove from heat and beat with a wooden spoon until you have a thick paste. Leave to cool for 5 minutes.

3 Beat the eggs, and pour a little into the pan, then beat again till smooth. Continue beating in the eggs a little at a time until the paste is thick and glossy. Stir in the cheese.

4 Put the paste in a large piping bag fitted with a ½ inch/1 cm piping tube. Pipe a wiggly line of paste onto the baking sheet, about 5–6 inches/12–15 cm long. Make nine more shapes (or however many you have mixture for) in the same way, spacing them slightly apart.

5 Cut out ½ inch/1 cm wide strips of green pepper. Cut across the strips to make small triangles. Rest these gently over the paste for snake markings. Bake for 20–25 minutes until risen and deep golden in color.

6 While baking, cut very thin strips from the red pepper, each about 1¼ inches/3 cm long for tongues. Cut a little fork into the end of each.

7 Once the pastries are finished baking, remove from the oven and leave to cool. Use the tip of a knife to cut a small slit into the end of each pastry and push the tongues in place. Cut the raisins into smaller pieces and push these in place for eyes.

TOP TIP

As you get more practiced with the piping bag, try putting a little more pressure on it to create a bigger snake head and trailing it off at the other end for the tail.

GOBLET OF FIRE CHILI DIP

 SERVES 4   **30 MINS**   **30 MINS**

Everyone is shocked when the Goblet of Fire spits out Harry Potter's name in the fourth movie. But rules are rules in the wizarding world, and it's not long before the young Gryffindor is facing a series of tasks that make his hair stand on end. This delicious fiery dip will also blow your socks off. For fun, try adding your own name to the accompanying cheese.

FOR THE DIP

2 tbsp olive oil

1 large onion, chopped

1 red chili, chopped

2 cans (14 oz/400 g each) chopped tomatoes

1 tbsp brown sugar

4 tbsp sun-dried tomato pesto

3 tbsp chopped cilantro/coriander

TO FINISH

4 mozzarella cheese slices

Natural brown food coloring

3 cups/175–200 g mixed blue corn and plain tortilla chips

SPECIAL EQUIPMENT

Fine paintbrush

1 Heat the oil in a large saucepan and gently fry the onion for 5 minutes. Add the chili, tomatoes, and brown sugar and heat until simmering. Continue to cook for about 25 minutes until the mixture is thick and jammy. Stir in the pesto and cilantro and remove from the heat.

2 Cut or tear the cheese slices into shapes resembling the burnt paper that shows the four names thrown from the Goblet of Fire (see Magical Fact below). Use the brown food coloring and fine paintbrush to write the names onto the cheese and color around the edges of the cheese so they look like they're charred from the fire.

3 Reheat the chili dip if preferred—it's good served hot or cold. Transfer to a small, deep pot. Serve surrounded by the tortilla chips and cheese slices.

TOP TIP

A substance in chili called capsaicin can sometimes cause a burning sensation in your hands after touching. We suggest wearing surgical or rubber gloves to prevent this.

MAGICAL FACT

The four names selected for the Triwizard Tournament are:

CEDRIC DIGGORY

VIKTOR KRUM

FLEUR DELACOUR

HARRY POTTER

LIGHTNING BOLT CHEESE BITES

 **MAKES 24** **40 MINS** **12-15 MINS**

These mini savory bites are shaped like Harry Potter's famous lightning bolt scar, which he unwittingly acquired after Lord Voldemort attacked him as a baby. Cheesy and filling, they make a tasty lunch or teatime treat or perhaps a snack to nibble while you're doing your homework. You wouldn't want to get on the wrong side of Professor Snape, now would you?

1½ cups/190 g all-purpose/plain flour

Good pinch of salt

1 stick/110 g unsalted butter, firm, diced

¾ cup/90 g finely grated cheddar cheese

1 large egg yolk

1 tsp mild chili powder

Beaten egg, to glaze

1 Preheat the oven to 375°F/190°C/gas mark 5. Line a large baking sheet with parchment paper. Put the flour, salt, and butter in a bowl and rub the butter in with your fingertips until the mixture resembles bread crumbs. Stir in the cheese and egg yolk and stir with a round-bladed knife until the mixture comes together to form a firm dough. Mold into a flat square shape.

2 Turn the dough out onto a lightly floured surface and roll out to a square measuring slightly larger than 9 inches/23 cm. Trim the edges to neaten. Cut lengthways into four even-sized strips. Cut across the dough at 1½ inch/4 cm intervals so that you finish up with 24 rectangles. Cut each rectangle diagonally in half.

3 To shape each lightning bolt, take the two halves of a rectangle and reposition them on the baking sheet so the points face away from each other and two of the long sides meet. Push the pieces firmly together so they don't fall apart after baking. Repeat with the remaining pieces.

4 Brush the bolts with beaten egg and use your fingers to sprinkle the chili powder in a fine dusting. Bake for 12-15 minutes until pale golden. Leave to cool on the baking sheet.

 **TOP TIP**

Follow this diagram—it shows you how to cut and position your dough to create your lightning bolt shapes.

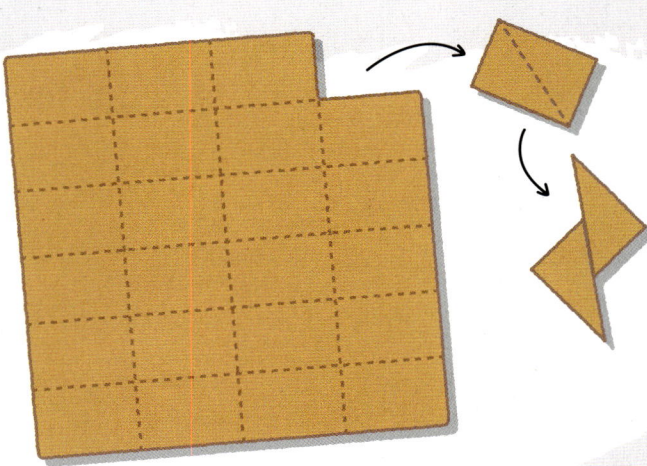

TOP TIP

If you make this ahead of time to be ready for lunch or supper, position the dill sprigs just before you eat so they don't wilt.

PROFESSOR SPROUT'S ZINGY-SPRINGY HERBOLOGY PATCH

Create your own delicious version of the Greenhouse Three classroom, where Harry and his fellow students have their always-entertaining Herbology lessons with Professor Pomona Sprout. Best assembled on a flat square plate or clean board, this colorful and healthy platter is a great way to make your veggies fun to eat. Just be thankful we haven't included any shrieking Mandrakes!

2 cans (7 oz/200 g each) tuna, drained

½ cup/120 g mayonnaise

2 tbsp chopped dill, optional

1½ cups/140 g rye or pumpernickel bread crumbs

TO FINISH

5 scallions/spring onions

5-6 baby carrots

Several sprigs fresh dill

1 large broccoli floret

1 large cauliflower floret

6-8 button mushrooms

SPECIAL EQUIPMENT

Small metal skewer

1 Put the tuna, mayonnaise, and dill, if using, in a bowl and mix well until thoroughly combined. Turn the mixture out onto a flat plate or board and spread evenly into a rectangle that measures about 10 x 8 inches/25 x 20 cm, or a similar size that fits the surface. Scatter with the bread crumbs.

2 Cut the root ends off the scallions and cut their lengths down to 2½ inches/6 cm. Use the tip of a sharp knife to make 1 inch/2.5 cm slits into the thin ends. Place in a bowl of iced water.

3 Cut a little slice from the thin ends of the carrots so they stand upright. Push the tip of a skewer into the stalk ends to make a hole. Press a little dill sprig into each hole. Arrange the carrots in a row on your plate.

4 Cut or break the broccoli and cauliflower florets into much smaller pieces. Drain the scallions. Arrange the vegetables and mushrooms in rows on either side of the carrots.

MAGICAL FACT

Professor Sprout is portrayed by Miriam Margolyes, who later played another witch in the stage musical *Wicked*.

TOP TIP

★

Not sure what to serve pickles with? It's best to keep it simple and dish them up with your favorite soft or hard cheese and some nice crusty bread. Or, if you feel more adventurous, try with burgers or salmon fillets, or scatter onto salads.

THE CURIOUS CUISINE OF KNOCKTURN ALLEY

SERVES 6 · **30 MINS** · **5 MINS**

Located just around the corner from Diagon Alley, Knockturn Alley is a dodgy place frequented by Dark wizards. You can find all kinds of sinister items on sale there including flesh-eating slug repellent and cursed necklaces. Crikey! While these sweet pickled beans might look like something you'd see in the front window of Borgin and Burkes, they're actually irresistibly good.

2 tbsp yellow or black mustard seeds

1 lb 2 oz/500 g green beans, ends trimmed

Large handful of dill sprigs

2 cups/500 ml white wine vinegar

¾ cup/150 g granulated sugar

½ cup/120 ml water

SPECIAL EQUIPMENT

2 screw-top or clip-top preserving jars, each with a capacity of about 2½ cups/600 ml

1 Heat a small saucepan and tip in the mustard seeds. Heat briefly until the seeds start to pop. Leave to cool.

2 Pack the beans and dill sprigs into the preserving jars so the dill shows around the sides of the glass. You might find this easier if the jar is on its side with a cloth underneath so the jar doesn't slip around. Scatter in the mustard seeds as you go.

3 Put the vinegar, sugar, and ½ cup/120 ml water into the saucepan and heat gently until the sugar has dissolved. Pour into the jars until the beans are covered. Secure the lids and store in the fridge for at least 24 hours. They will also keep for up to a month.

WHY NOT TRY THIS?

If you like the idea of sweet pickles, you might want to make this too:

PICKLED CUCUMBER

Use the recipe above but pack the jars full of sliced cucumber instead of beans. You could also add some thinly sliced red onions to induce flavor and make the jars look interesting.

DID YOU KNOW?

You can also pickle hard-boiled eggs!

SNACKS

Hogsmeade Festive Popcorn Treats

 SERVES 6   **10 MINS**   **10 MINS**

If you want to feel Christmassy, then Hogsmeade is the place for you. The only all-wizarding village in the UK, the crooked shops and taverns in its even more crooked streets are permanently snow-covered during the winter months, and sell all manner of warming fare, including Butterbeer. This popcorn with a twist will have you feeling festive in no time, especially if eaten while watching your favorite holiday movie. And it takes just minutes to make!

GF

3 thin slices of bacon, chopped

½ cup/60 g finely grated cheddar or Parmesan cheese

1 tbsp vegetable oil

¼ cup/50 g popping corn

Good pinch of black pepper (optional)

SPECIAL EQUIPMENT
Paper or plastic food bag

1 Cook the bacon in a dry frying pan for about 8 minutes until very crispy. Leave to cool. Transfer to a paper or plastic food bag and crush with a rolling pin to crumble it into very small pieces. Mix with the cheese.

2 Briefly heat the oil in a large saucepan. Tip in the corn, cover with a lid, and shake the pan so the kernels are coated in oil. Cook until the kernels pop.

3 Once the popping has almost stopped, remove the pan from the heat and let stand for 2 minutes until the popping completely stops. Sprinkle with the bacon and cheese and a little black pepper if you like. Stir lightly to combine and serve.

TRY THESE OTHER MAGICAL FLAVORS!

⭐ Use different cheeses like finely grated Halloumi, Gruyère, or crumbled feta.

V For a veggie variation, omit the bacon and add a handful of chopped herbs such as chives, cilantro, or thyme.

⭐ Drizzle with melted milk chocolate or white chocolate.

⭐ Simply sprinkle with salt or sugar.

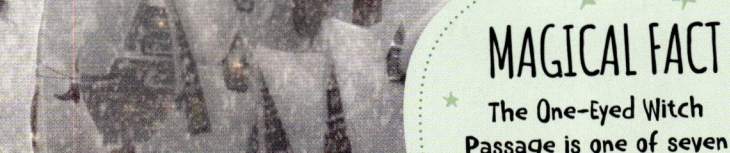

MAGICAL FACT
The One-Eyed Witch Passage is one of seven secret tunnels in and around Hogwarts. This one is especially handy, though, as it leads directly to the cellar beneath Honeydukes Sweet Shop in Hogsmeade.

ARAGOG'S CHILDREN DOUGH BALLS

🍴 MAKES 6   ⏰ 45 MINS PLUS PROOFING   🔥 10-12 MINS

Even the youngest cooks in your household can have fun assembling these little spidery treats. They're shaped to look like the many (and very hungry) children of Aragog—the enormous, eight-legged Acromantula who lives in the Forbidden Forest and who regards all humans except Hagrid as prey. Moist and filling, with the raisins adding a burst of fruity flavor, these delectable dough balls will certainly leave you in a spin.

FOR THE DOUGH

2 cups/250 g white bread flour

4 tbsp finely grated Parmesan cheese

1 tsp active dry yeast

½ tsp salt

2 tbsp tomato paste

2 tbsp olive oil

½ cup/120 ml warm water

TO FINISH

1 carrot

Small handful raisins

1 large bag of pretzel sticks or Twiglets

1   To make the dough, put the flour, Parmesan, yeast, salt, tomato paste, and oil in a bowl. Add ½ cup/120 ml warm water and mix well with a round-bladed knife until the mixture comes together to form a dough. (Add a little more water if the dough is dry and crumbly.) Turn out onto a floured surface and knead for 10 minutes until the dough is completely smooth and elastic. Place in a lightly oiled bowl, cover with plastic wrap, and leave in a warm place for about an hour or until the dough has doubled in size.

2   Line a baking sheet with parchment paper. Punch the dough to deflate it and turn out onto a floured surface. Divide into six even-sized pieces.

3   Preheat the oven to 400°F/200°C/gas mark 6. Take one piece of the dough and cut off a third. Shape both into balls and place side by side on the baking sheet. The smaller piece of dough will form the front of the spider. Make five more spider shapes in the same way using the remaining dough. Cover loosely with plastic wrap and leave in a warm place for 20 minutes.

4   Remove the plastic wrap and place the dough in the oven. Bake 10-12 minutes until risen. The dough balls should sound hollow when tapped on the underside. Transfer to a wire rack to cool.

5   Cut a thin, lengthways slice from the carrot. Cut thin, pointed shards from the slice for fangs. Select plenty of even-sized lengths of pretzel sticks or Twiglets, each around 2½ inches/6 cm long. If necessary break them down to size.

6   Using the tip of a sharp knife, make little slits into the front of one of the bakes and push a couple of raisins into the slits for eyes. Make more slits and push in the carrot fangs. Make four slits on either side and push the pretzel sticks or Twiglets into place. Assemble the remaining spiders in the same way.

MAGICAL FACT

Harry Potter actor Daniel Radcliffe admits to being "genuinely terrified" the first time he saw a full-scale model of Aragog. We don't blame him—Hagrid's former pet is the size of a small elephant, with each of its eight legs nearly 20 feet/6 meters in length.

Sir Cadogan's Sword Kebabs

 MAKES 4 **20 MINS** **6-8 MINS**

Inspired by the sword of Sir Cadogan, the preposterously brave wizard and knight who resides in a portrait at the end of the Divination corridor at Hogwarts (when he's not guarding the Gryffindor Common Room or off on one of his crazy quests, anyway), these tasty little fruit kebabs make the perfect after-dinner treat. Colorful, fun, and easy to assemble, they can be eaten as they are or with scoops of soft and creamy vanilla ice cream.

I thick slice cut from a large pineapple

2 kiwi fruit

½ small mango

I banana

4 large green grapes

4 small black or red grapes

4 large and 4 small strawberries

3-4 tbsp ready-made gluten-free caramel sauce

SPECIAL EQUIPMENT

4 skewers (wooden or metal)

Pastry brush

Griddle pan, optional

1 Cut four 2½ x ½ inch/6 x 1 cm rectangles from the pineapple and thread onto the skewers until about 3 inches/7.5 cm from the ends. Cut four chunky cubes from the kiwi fruit and mango and four thick slices from the banana.

2 Thread all the fruit onto the skewers, with the smaller fruit such as the grapes and small strawberries nearest the tip.

3 Put the caramel sauce in a small bowl and soften in the microwave for a few seconds. Place the kebabs on a foil-lined baking sheet if using a regular grill, and preheat the grill. Alternatively, preheat a griddle pan.

4 Brush the kebabs with half the caramel sauce and cook for 6-8 minutes, turning once and brushing with the remaining sauce.

"What villains are these that trespass on my private lands? Who dares challenge Sir Cadogan?"

—SIR CADOGAN
Harry Potter and the Prisoner of Azkaban

TOP TIP
✦ ★ ★ ✦

A ridged griddle pan is great for giving ingredients a professional-looking "seared" finish. It's best to get the pan really hot before you add the kebabs.

GOLDEN PEANUT SNITCHES

 MAKES 12   **30 MINS** 🗓 **3-5 MINS**

Channel your inner Seeker and catch the Golden Snitch again and again with this fun and filling recipe. You probably don't have a Nimbus 2000 or a Firebolt lying around, so a fork or your fingers will have to do. With a peanut and chili-infused body and toasted bread for wings, these little balls of fire will have you cheering loudly—just like the noisy Gryffindor students at a Quidditch game when Harry is chasing the Snitch.

V

½ cup/150 g crunchy peanut butter

½ cup/30 g fresh bread crumbs

2 tbsp chopped cilantro/coriander

1 mild red chili, finely chopped

2 tsp light brown sugar

4-6 slices thinly sliced white bread

TO SERVE:

Sweet chili dipping sauce

SPECIAL EQUIPMENT

Fine metal skewer or toothpick

1 Put the peanut butter, bread crumbs, cilantro, chili, and sugar in a bowl and mix well until you have a thick, evenly combined paste. Use the back of a wooden spoon or your hands to do this. Turn the paste out onto the surface and pack it into a log shape. Cut across into 12 evenly sized pieces. Roll each into a firm ball between the palms of your hands.

2 Trace and cut out the wing templates (see page 120). Flatten a slice of bread by rolling firmly with a rolling pin. Place the templates on the bread and cut around using kitchen scissors. Make close cuts all along one side as shown on the template. Make 23 more wings in the same way. Preheat your oven's grill or broiler to high. Place the bread wings on a baking sheet or grill rack and toast lightly on both sides. Watch closely as they can burn quickly!

3 Use a fine metal skewer or toothpick to make holes in the peanut balls and push the pointed tips of the bread wings into them. Serve on a platter or board with a small bowl of chili dipping sauce.

MAGICAL FACT

In *Harry Potter and the Sorcerer's Stone* (known as *Harry Potter and the Philosopher's Stone* in the UK), Harry becomes the youngest player in a century to play Quidditch for a Hogwarts house team. We later learn that Harry's father was also a Seeker.

MEALS

"In the old days, I used to throw together the occasional supper party. Select a student or two. Would you be game?"

— PROFESSOR SLUGHORN —

Looking for mealtime inspiration? From hearty stews to Scotch eggs with a veggie twist, this section is packed with recipes that'll make your mouth water.

A Pie Fit for the Weasleys

If there's one thing the redheaded Weasley family love almost as much as one another, it's food—and this scrumptious meat and veggie pie would definitely be a big hit in The Burrow. Not only is it large enough to feed a family of seven (nine if Charlie and Bill are visiting), it's bursting with flavor and, best of all, can be assembled in advance. All you have to do is pop it in the oven.

FOR THE FILLING

4 cups/1 kg diced turkey breast or thigh meat, or a mixture of both

Good pinch of salt

Good pinch of black pepper

½ stick/55 g butter

3 onions, chopped

3 large carrots, diced

4 tbsp all-purpose/plain flour

2½ cups/600 ml chicken stock

1 cup/150 g diced ham

¾ cup/75 g dried cranberries

2 tsp dried thyme

Handful of parsley, chopped

TO FINISH

2¼ lb/1 kg puff pastry

Beaten egg, to glaze

SPECIAL EQUIPMENT

Large shallow pie dish

Baking beans, or dried beans (see Top Tip)

1 To make the filling, put the turkey in a bowl and season with salt and pepper. Use your hands or a wooden spoon to do this. Melt half the butter in a large saucepan and fry half the meat for 5 minutes until lightly browned. Lift out onto a plate, add the remaining turkey, and fry until browned. Add to the plate.

2 Melt the remaining butter and fry the onions and carrots for 5 minutes. Return the turkey to the pan and sprinkle with the flour. Cook, stirring with a wooden spoon for 3 minutes. Add the stock, ham, cranberries, thyme, and parsley and heat until simmering. Cover with a lid and cook gently for 30 minutes. Leave to cool.

3 Preheat the oven to 400°F/200°C/gas mark 6. Roll out half the pastry on a lightly floured surface until it is big enough to fit the pie dish and overhang the edges without stretching the pastry too much. Press into the dish to fit and trim off the overhanging edges with kitchen scissors. This needn't be neat—think busy Mrs. Weasley! Reserve the trimmings.

4 Prick the base of the pastry all over with a fork, about 20 times. Press a sheet of parchment paper into the dish and fill with baking beans. This will stop the pastry from rising and shrinking away from the sides as it cooks. Bake for 25 minutes. Remove from the oven, lift out the beans and paper, and return the pie to the oven for an additional 5 minutes.

Continues on page 48

TOP TIP ★

Baking beans are small, heat-conducting ceramic beans that are available from kitchenware stores. Alternatively, you can use any dried beans such as navy beans or red kidney beans—just remember, once you've used them as baking beans they won't be edible. Instead, put them in a labeled container and reserve them for the next time you make a pie.

DID YOU KNOW?

Baking a pastry case with baking beans is known as "baking blind." It's used for pies and tarts where the base needs to be cooked separately first to ensure an even bake. It's also used in recipes where the filling is not cooked at all.

5. Once the base has been removed from the oven, spoon the filling into the pastry case. Brush the pastry edges with a beaten egg. Reserve a quarter of the remaining pastry. Roll out the rest until large enough to completely cover the pie. Lift this over the filling and press down around the rim with your fingers to seal it to the pastry base. Trim off the overhanging edges with kitchen scissors and brush the pastry with more beaten egg.

6. Roll out the reserved pastry and the trimmings. Cut out large "PIE" letters and position on top of the pastry. Using the tip of a sharp knife, make deep crosses all over the surface of the pie. Use the trimmings to cut a patchwork of irregular squares and rectangles and arrange these around the edges of the pie. Brush the decorations with beaten egg and bake the pie for 45 minutes until deep golden in color.

"Harry! Thank heavens you're all right. Bit peaky, but I'm afraid dinner will have to wait until after the meeting's finished. No time to explain. Straight upstairs, first door on the left . . ."

—MRS. WEASLEY
HARRY POTTER AND THE ORDER OF THE PHOENIX

GLEAMING GRINGOTTS GOLD BARS

 SERVES 4 **20 MINS** 🍳 **5-10 MINS**

The only wizarding bank in the UK, Gringotts is protected by spells, enchantments, and even dragons. "Ain't no safer place, not one, except perhaps Hogwarts," says Hagrid to Harry in *Harry Potter and the Sorcerer's Stone*. You'll need similar levels of security to keep your family and friends away from these precious gold bars, which are actually rich and delicious fish fingers. Serve with the sweet and tangy gold sauce for added bite!

FOR THE DIP

I tsp ground turmeric

I tbsp boiling water

¼ cup/60 g mayonnaise

¼ cup/60 g Greek-style yogurt

2 scallions/spring onions, chopped

I tbsp mango chutney

FOR THE FISH

I lb/450 g skinned cod or
   haddock fillet

2 tbsp all-purpose/plain flour

I egg, beaten

I cup/100 g fresh bread crumbs

A little vegetable oil, for frying

1. Combine the turmeric with I tbsp boiling water in a small bowl. Stir in the mayonnaise, yogurt, scallions, and mango chutney and reserve for dipping.

2. Cut the fish into ½ inch/I cm–wide strips, making them as uniform in size as you can. Sprinkle the flour onto a plate and season with a little salt and pepper. Beat the egg on another plate and scatter the bread crumbs onto a third.

3. Add the fish to the flour plate and turn them in the flour until lightly coated. Take a few pieces of fish at a time and dip them first in the egg to coat and then into the bread crumbs, turning them until completely coated. Repeat with the remaining pieces of fish.

4. Heat a thin layer of oil in a frying pan and fry half the fish bars for I–2 minutes on each side until golden. Lift these out onto a plate lined with paper towels while you cook the remainder in the same way. Stack the fish bars on a plate and serve with the sauce for dipping.

SNACK OR SUPPER?

These tasty savory bites can be served as a snack just as they are. For more of a meal, try them with french fries and a bowl of leafy salad.

MAGICAL FACT

The beautiful banking hall at Gringotts was designed not only to look impressive, but also to make the goblins who work there seem smaller, with towering marble columns and raised desks.

START-OF-TERM PLATTER

An eleven-year-old Harry Potter can't quite believe his eyes when he experiences his first start-of-term feast. The four house tables in the Great Hall are filled with food, from plates overflowing with chicken drumsticks, fries, and veggies to every mouth-watering dessert you can think of. This recipe shows you how to create a pizza-based platter worthy of Hogwarts. Just make sure to tell your guests to arrive hungry!

FOR THE PIZZA BASE

4 cups/500 g white bread flour

2 tsp active dry yeast

1½ tsp salt

3 tbsp olive oil

1⅓ cups/340 ml warm water

TO FINISH

¾ cup/175 g pizza sauce/tomato sauce

12 mozzarella cheese slices

1 tbsp clear honey

2 tsp grainy/wholegrain mustard

6 small chicken drumsticks

1½ cups/275 g cocktail sausages

2 cups/200 g frozen french fries

6 lamb cutlets

1 cup/125 g peas

6 small pieces corn on the cob

6 cutlet frills (see Top Tip)

1   To make the pizza base, put the flour, yeast, salt, and oil in a bowl. Add 1⅓ cups/300 ml warm water and mix well with a round-bladed knife until the mixture comes together to form a dough. Add a little more water if the dough is dry and crumbly. Turn out onto a floured surface and knead for 10 minutes until the dough is completely smooth and elastic. Place in a lightly oiled bowl, cover with plastic wrap, and leave in a warm place for about 1 hour or until the dough has doubled in size.

2   Preheat the oven to 425°F/220°C/gas mark 7. Punch the dough to deflate it and turn out onto a floured surface. Roll out to a rectangle measuring about 15¾ x 12 inches/40 x 30 cm. Transfer the dough to a large, floured baking sheet, pulling and stretching it back into shape on the baking sheet. Spread almost to the edges with pizza sauce and arrange the cheese slices on top. Leave in a warm place while cooking the toppings.

3   Mix together the honey and mustard and spread over the chicken pieces. Place in a large roasting tin and bake on the top shelf of the oven for 20 minutes. Add the sausages and fries and return to the oven for 30 minutes. At the same time place the pizza on the lower shelf and bake for 25-30 minutes until risen and golden.

4   When your kitchen timer has about 10 minutes left, heat a dry frying pan and fry the lamb cutlets for 4 minutes on each side. Bring a saucepan of water to boil and cook the corn for 5 minutes. Add the peas and cook for an additional minute. Drain through a colander. Push toothpicks into the ends of the corncobs.

5   Slide the pizza onto a large serving board and arrange the corn, fries, lamb, chicken, peas, and sausages in rows on top. Decorate the lamb tips with cutlet frills before serving.

TOP TIP

Instead of buying cutlet frills, why not make your own? For each frill, cut out a 3 x 2½ inch/7.5 x 6 cm rectangle of white paper and fold in half lengthways. Using paper scissors make deep, close cuts from the folded edge toward the open edge. Open out, fold in the opposite direction, and roll the short ends to meet. Secure in place with sticky tape.

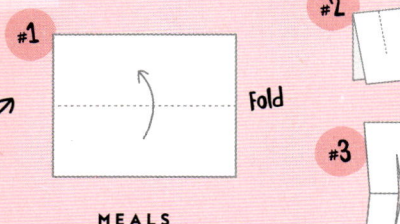

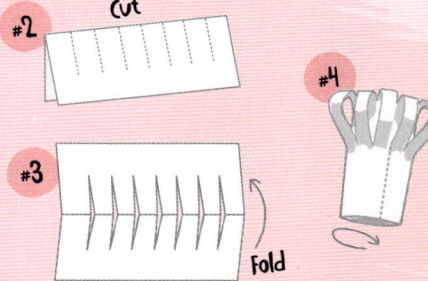

DID YOU KNOW?

You can make your own cocktail sausages from regular-sized ones. Simply pinch the middle of the sausage between your thumb and finger until they meet, then twist the two halves in opposite directions to make two mini sausages. Cut through with kitchen scissors.

KNIGHT BUS

TOP TIP The length and width of the bread loaf need to be the same dimensions as the meat loaf when cut into three rectangles. If you can only find a bigger loaf, cut it down to size before you start.

STAN SHUNPIKE'S KNIGHT BUS IN A BUN

 SERVES 6   **1–1½ HOURS**   **50 MINS**

What do you get if you combine three layers of meat loaf, thick "doorstops" of bread, and other yummy ingredients? A fun version of the Knight Bus, that's what—the magical, triple-decker transport that whizzes around the UK picking up stranded witches and wizards, including a newly homeless Harry. With purple windows and its own sign, our version looks pretty realistic. In fact, you can almost hear conductor Stan Shunpike saying: "Take her away, Ern!"

FOR THE MEAT LOAF

3 cups/750 g lean ground/minced beef

8 thin slices of bacon, chopped

1½ cups/150 g bread crumbs

1 large onion, finely chopped

2 tsp dried oregano

1 large egg, beaten

2 tbsp grainy/wholegrain mustard

Good pinch of salt

Good pinch of black pepper

TO FINISH

1 tbsp vegetable oil

2 onions, thinly sliced

4 tbsp mayonnaise

Purple natural food coloring

4 thin slices zucchini/courgette

4 small pieces black olive

4 slices cooked beet/beetroot

1 small uncut white loaf, measuring about 6 inches/15 cm long, 3½ inches/9 cm wide, and 5 inches/12 cm deep

7 cheddar cheese slices, or any other burger cheese

Small bunch arugula/rocket

SPECIAL EQUIPMENT

12 x 9 inch/30 x 23 cm straight-sided roasting tin or baking tin

Small paper or plastic piping bag

1 Preheat the oven to 375°F/190°C/gas mark 5. Line the base and sides of the roasting tin or baking tin with a large rectangle of parchment paper so that it comes about 2 inches/5 cm up the sides. Crease the paper into the corners.

2 Combine all the ingredients for the meat loaf in a large bowl, add a little salt and pepper, and mix together well. (This is easiest done with your hands.) Tip the mixture into the tin and spread level, making sure it goes right into the corners. Bake for 40 minutes.

3 While cooking, heat the oil in a frying pan and fry the onions for 8 minutes or until deep golden. Beat the mayonnaise in a small bowl with a little purple food coloring. Position a slice of zucchini and a piece of black olive onto each beet slice for the wheels. Cut a 2½ x 1¼ inch/6 x 3 cm rectangle from one of the cheese slices.

4 Using a bread knife, slice the crusty top off the bread for the roof, then cut the loaf horizontally into three thick slices. When your meat loaf is cooked, pour off any liquid from the meat loaf and lift out of the tin. Cut the meat loaf widthways into three even-sized rectangles, trimming them down if necessary so they're the same size as the bread slices. Place the bread base on a baking sheet, add a rectangle of meat loaf, and cover with two cheese slices and a thin layer of fried onions, followed by a layer of arugula leaves. Cover with a second layer of bread. Continue layering the ingredients in this way, finishing with the roof. Return to the oven for 10 more minutes.

5 Carefully transfer the bus to a serving board and position a wheel at each corner, securing in place with a dot of mayonnaise. Add the cheese rectangle to the front of the bus with another dot of mayonnaise. Place the mayonnaise in the piping bag and snip off a small tip so it can be piped in a thin line. Use it to pipe windows around the sides and write "KNIGHT BUS" onto the cheese rectangle.

TOP TIP

Traditional Scotch eggs are wrapped in sausage meat. You can use a good-quality sausage meat instead of the haggis, or try vegetarian sausage meat instead. Don't forget to add the scallions for a nice burst of savoriness.

McGonagall's Very Scottish Eggs

 MAKES 6   **1 HOUR**   🍳 **30 MINS**

Serve these scrumptious Scotch eggs to your family and friends, and it'll definitely be 10 points for Gryffindor! Wrapped in vegetarian haggis—not the usual spicy meat variety that Professor McGonagall would remember from growing up in the Scottish Highlands—these appetizing eggs are fun, flavorful, and filling. You and your family are sure to gobble down the lot.

7 large eggs

1 lb 2 oz/500 g vegetarian haggis

1 bunch scallions/spring onions, finely chopped

All-purpose/plain flour, for dusting

¾ cup/75 g bread crumbs

Dipping sauce of your choice

1 Put six of the eggs in a saucepan and cover with just-boiled water from the kettle. Return the eggs to a boil and cook for 6 minutes. Carefully drain off the water and fill the pan with cold water. The cold water stops the eggs cooking any further. Leave the eggs to cool.

2 Put the haggis in a bowl with half the scallions and mix the two ingredients together. This is easiest done with your hands. Turn out onto the surface and pat into a cake. Cut into six even-sized wedges. Take one wedge and flatten it out between the palms of your hands until it is as thin as you can make it without it falling apart. Repeat with the remaining pieces.

3 Sprinkle a little flour on a plate. Mix together the bread crumbs and remaining scallions on another plate. Beat the remaining egg with a fork on a third plate.

Continues on page 58

COOKING BASICS

HOW TO BOIL AN EGG!

Eggs can be soft-, medium-, or hard-boiled. The cooking time in step 1 of this recipe gives a medium-boiled (slightly soft) egg.

For a SOFT-BOILED BREAKFAST EGG (for dipping pieces of toast or bread), boil the eggs for 3 minutes.

For a HARD-BOILED EGG (for salads, sandwiches, or lunch boxes), allow 9–10 minutes.

4 Preheat the oven to 400°F/200°C/gas mark 6. Line a baking sheet with parchment paper. Remove the eggs from the water and peel. Roll them in the flour until lightly dusted. Roll one dusted, hard-boiled egg in the beaten egg until coated in a thin film. Lift a piece of haggis in the palm of your hand, place the egg in the center, and carefully wrap the haggis around the egg. This will take a little time as the haggis might crack, but keep patching it together and smoothing the mixture around the egg until evenly covered. Repeat with the remaining eggs.

5 Roll the haggis-wrapped eggs once again in the flour, then in the beaten egg, and finally in the bread crumbs. Place on the baking sheet and bake for 25 minutes until golden. Serve warm or cold, and you can pair with the dipping sauce of your choice.

> ## "Why is it when something happens, it is always you three?"
> —PROFESSOR MCGONAGALL
> *HARRY POTTER AND THE HALF-BLOOD PRINCE*

MAGICAL FACT

Professor McGonagall shares her first name with the Roman goddess Minerva, patron of wisdom, justice, and strategic warfare. Rather fitting, don't you think?

DID YOU KNOW?

You can always tell when an egg has been boiled for too long. When halved, the egg yolk will have a thin bluish/black ring around it.

GREAT HALL SHEPHERD'S PIE

 SERVES 6 30 MINS 1¾ HOURS

After a Quidditch training session in the depths of winter or a particularly hair-raising Care of Magical Creatures lesson with Hagrid, there's nothing better than a warming meal in the Great Hall. One of Harry's favorites, this goodness-packed shepherd's pie is the perfect dish for when you're in need of a similar hearty boost. It's scrumptious, filling, and just the ticket!

GF

2¼ lb/1 kg potatoes, cut into chunks

½ stick/55 g butter

2 onions, roughly chopped

3 carrots, roughly chopped

2 cups/500 g ground/minced lamb

14 oz/400 g can baked beans

¾ cup/175 ml lamb or chicken stock

Good pinch of salt

Good pinch of black pepper

Large handful parsley, chopped

3 tbsp tomato paste

A little milk

1 Cook the potatoes in boiling, lightly salted water for 15 minutes until tender. Melt about a third of the butter in a large saucepan and gently fry the onions and carrots for 5 minutes. Add the lamb and cook for an additional 5 minutes, breaking it up with a wooden spoon.

2 Stir in the baked beans, stock, parsley, and tomato paste and heat until simmering. Cook for 30 minutes, stirring occasionally until the mixture has thickened slightly.

3 While the meat is cooking, drain the potatoes and return to the saucepan. Add the remaining butter and a dash of milk, and mash the potatoes well until completely smooth.

4 Season the lamb to taste with salt and pepper. Carefully turn the mixture into a large baking dish. Preheat the oven to 425°F/220°C/gas mark 7.

5 Spoon or pipe the potato over the lamb in an even layer (see Top Tip). Bake in the oven for 15 minutes. Reduce the oven temperature to 350°F/180°C/gas mark 4 and bake for an additional 30 minutes until the potatoes are golden.

TOP TIP

If you want to be a little clever with the potato topping, pipe it onto the filling in big starry swirls instead. To do this, put the mashed potatoes in a large piping bag fitted with a large star piping tube and pipe large stars over the filling. Piping takes a bit of practice, but it's a great skill to learn.

MAGICAL FACT

Look closely at the walls of the Great Hall and you'll spot gargoyles shaped like the four house mascots (raven, badger, lion, and snake) holding up flaming torches.

TOP TIP

⚬ ★ ★ ⚬

This recipe is particularly good for perfecting chopping skills! Prepare the cabbage, zucchini, and onion in advance when you might have more time for cutting them finely.

WHOMPING WILLOW SOUP

 SERVES 2–4   30 MINS   20 MINS

One look at this appetizing soup and you can almost imagine poor Ron and Harry trapped in Mr. Weasley's modified Ford Anglia as the Whomping Willow attempts to thump and bump them out of its branches. Here, we've replaced the infamous tree's bark with thin strips of zucchini and cabbage, which you can arrange creatively over the soup when it's served. There's enough for four as a starter, or two for a hearty main course.

V **VG**

2 cups/500 ml vegetable stock

I large zucchini/courgette

2–3 large green cabbage leaves

2 tbsp vegetable oil

I onion, chopped

3 cloves garlic, crushed

¼ cup/75 g chunky peanut butter

I tbsp finely grated fresh ginger root

3 tbsp soy sauce

I4 oz/400 g can black beans, drained

1 Heat the stock in a saucepan, add the zucchini, and cook gently for 5 minutes. Transfer the zucchini to a board, reserving the stock.

2 Roll up the cabbage leaves tightly and cut across into thin slices with a knife. If the leaves have a thick central core, it's easier to cut this away first. Cut the zucchini lengthways into very thin slices. Cut the slices across into thin lengths, as fine as you can make them.

3 Heat the oil in a large saucepan and gently fry the onion and garlic for 5 minutes until the onion has softened. Stir in the peanut butter, ginger, and reserved stock and heat until the peanut butter has melted. Stir in the soy sauce and beans and cook gently for 5 minutes.

4 Add the cabbage and zucchini to the pan, pushing the vegetables down into the stock to soften. Cook gently for 3–4 minutes until soft. Ladle into bowls and serve.

"You have risked the exposure of our world. Not to mention the damage you inflicted on a Whomping Willow that's been on these grounds since before you were born!"

—PROFESSOR SNAPE
Harry Potter and the Chamber of Secrets

HAGRID'S HUGE & HEARTY STEW

 SERVES 4   30 MINS   2¼ HOURS

Hagrid isn't known for his cuisine, as anyone who's eaten his rock cakes will tell you! But if there's one thing the gentle half-giant is good at, we reckon, it's big, beefy stews—especially when the recipe is as easy to follow as this. Packed with meat and veggies, it's a flavorful, one-pot, comfort-food supper that young Gryffindors everywhere will adore (and older ones too).

I tbsp all-purpose/plain flour

Good pinch of salt

Good pinch of black pepper

1¾ cups/400 g beef stew meat or braising steak, cut into small dice

3 tbsp vegetable oil

3 large carrots, cut into small dice

2 onions, chopped

I leek, thinly sliced

2 cloves garlic, crushed

¼ cup/50 g pearl barley

3 cups/750 ml beef stock

I tbsp grainy/wholegrain mustard

Good handful parsley, chopped, plus extra to sprinkle

2 large baking potatoes, cut into small dice

1   Sprinkle the flour and a little salt and pepper onto a plate. Add the meat and turn in the flour until lightly dusted. Heat 2 tbsp of the oil in a large saucepan and fry half the meat until browned. This will take about 5 minutes. Lift out onto a plate while you brown the remaining meat and add to the plate.

2   Add the carrots, onions, leek, and garlic to the pan with the remaining oil and fry gently for 5 minutes. Return the meat to the pan with the pearl barley, stock, mustard, and parsley and heat until simmering. Reduce the heat to its lowest setting and cover with a lid. Cook gently for I hour. Add the potatoes to the pan and cook for an additional hour until the meat is very tender. Serve in bowls, sprinkled with extra parsley.

"Got something for ya! 'Fraid I might have sat on it at some point, but I imagine it'll taste fine just the same."

—HAGRID
Harry Potter and the Sorcerer's Stone

MAGICAL FACT

Not only was Robbie Coltrane Harry Potter author J. K. Rowling's first choice to play Hagrid, he was also the first adult actor cast in the entire movie series.

For a vegetarian option, use 5 cups/500 g halved mushrooms instead of the beef, flouring and seasoning as on the opposite page. Use vegetable stock instead of beef stock.

HEALTHY HOGWARTS HOUSE PASTA

 SERVES 4   10 MINS   15 MINS

Gryffindor, Ravenclaw, Hufflepuff, and Slytherin . . . all four Hogwarts houses are equally represented in this flavorsome and energy-boosting dish. We especially love this recipe because the shape of the pasta reminds us of the bow ties Harry and Ron begrudgingly wear to the Yule Ball. Feel free to mix up the ingredients when you give it a go—just remember to choose foods in the four house colors!

3 cups/200 g dried farfalle pasta

2 tbsp olive oil

2 cups/300 g eggplant/aubergine, diced

½ cup/50 g pepperoni, diced

1 yellow pepper, cut into small chunks

⅔ cup/100 g green beans, cut into short lengths

⅔ cup/150 ml vinaigrette dressing

1 Bring a large saucepan of lightly salted water to a boil and cook the pasta for 10–12 minutes, or until just tender.

2 While cooking, heat the oil in a frying pan and gently fry the eggplant for 8 minutes until softened and golden. Stir in the pepperoni and yellow pepper and cook for 2 minutes.

3 When your pasta has about two minutes left, add the beans to the pot to cook. Drain through a colander or large sieve and tip the cooked pasta and beans into a bowl. Stir in the fried ingredients and dressing and serve warm, or leave to cool for a lunch-box filler.

TOP TIP

You can easily make your own vinaigrette dressing by mixing the following ingredients in a small bowl:
6 tbsp olive oil,
2 tbsp wine vinegar,
2 tsp sugar,
1 tsp Dijon mustard,
and a little salt
and pepper.

DID YOU KNOW?

Farfalle pasta is also known as bow tie pasta because of its shape. In the Italian language, farfalle means "butterfly," which the pasta also resembles.

ORDER OF THE PHOENIX OVERNIGHT OATS

 SERVES 1   15 MINUTES, PLUS OVERNIGHT SOAKING

Like the Order of the Phoenix—the underground society first founded by Albus Dumbledore in the 1970s and then covertly resurrected by his friends a few decades later—this recipe is so good that you'll want to keep it a secret. It's actually a variation on Bircher Muesli, in which the oats are soaked overnight to make them soft and creamy. Just don't forget to do this before you go to bed!

1/3 cup/35 g rolled oats/porridge oats

1/2 cup/120 ml milk (or any dairy-free milk)

Good pinch of ground cinnamon

TO SERVE

1/2 apple or pear

Small handful of raisins or golden raisins/sultanas

1 tsp poppy seeds

2 tbsp pistachio nuts, finely chopped (see Top Tip)

3 raspberries, blackberries, or small strawberries

Honey to serve, optional

1 Put the oats, milk, and cinnamon in a breakfast bowl, cover, and leave in a cool place or the fridge overnight.

2 The next morning, grate the apple or pear into the bowl (there's no need to peel the fruit first). Stir in the raisins.

3 Use your fingers to sprinkle a spiral of poppy seeds over the oatmeal. Sprinkle the nuts between the poppy seeds and decorate the center with the soft fruit. Serve drizzled with a little honey if you like.

VE For a vegan option, use dairy-free milk, and maple syrup to replace the honey.

SOME OTHER TASTY TOPPINGS

Try any other seeds, chopped nuts, and fresh or dried fruit toppings in this recipe. Here are a few delicious combinations:

★ Sliced bananas tossed in lime juice and drizzled with maple syrup

★ Grapefruit segments, sprinkled with brown sugar and scattered with toasted hazelnuts

★ Fresh blueberries, flaked almonds, and a sprinkling of vanilla sugar

★ A swirl of yogurt and your favorite fruit jam

★ Dried cranberries, pumpkin seeds, and a little grated white chocolate

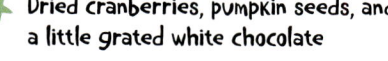

TOP TIP

❧ ★ ★ ❧

If you like, remove the brown skins from the pistachios before chopping to reveal more of their beautiful green color. Place the nuts in a heatproof bowl, cover with boiling water from the kettle, and leave for 2 minutes. Drain, then rub between layers of paper towels to loosen the skins. Peel away completely.

TRANSFIGURATION PANCAKES

 MAKES 6-8   30 MINS   10 MINS

In *Harry Potter and the Sorcerer's Stone*, Harry and Ron are stunned when the tabby cat sitting on Professor McGonagall's desk transforms into their very cross teacher. This type of spell is known as transfiguration, and it's where objects are changed from one thing into another. A little like these pancakes, which are golden on one side but dark when flipped. Perfect for breakfast or teatime with any of the toppings listed below.

FOR THE PANCAKES

I cup/125 g all-purpose/plain flour

I tsp baking powder

Good pinch of salt

2 tbsp granulated sugar

I large egg

²/₃ cup/150 ml milk

I tbsp cocoa powder

I tsp vanilla extract

Vegetable oil, for frying

TOPPINGS

Maple syrup or chocolate sauce

Whipped cream, pouring cream, or Greek-style yogurt

Raspberries, blueberries, peaches, mango, or pineapple

1 Put the flour and baking powder in a bowl with a pinch of salt and the sugar. Make a dip in the center and break the egg into it. Add a dash of the milk. Use a whisk to beat the egg and milk together, gradually working in the flour a little at a time. As the mixture thickens, add more milk until you have a thick, smooth batter. Spoon a third of the batter into a separate bowl and stir in the cocoa powder. Stir the vanilla extract into the remainder.

2 Heat a frying pan with a drizzle of the oil. Once the oil is hot, add a large spoonful of the vanilla batter so it spreads to about 3½ inches/9 cm in diameter. Add another spoonful on the other side of the pan. It's best to cook only a couple of pancakes at a time as they cook so quickly. After about a minute, once bubbles start to pop on the surface, turn the pancakes over with a palette knife or spatula. Place a smaller spoonful of the chocolate batter on top of each and spread to the edges with the back of a spoon.

3 Turn the pancakes again and cook for an additional 30 seconds. Lift out onto a plate. Heat a dash more oil and cook the remaining batter in the same way. Serve with any of the toppings.

TOP TIP

To make a delicious chocolate sauce to pour over the pancakes, put ²/₃ cup/100 g milk chocolate chips or chopped chocolate in a small saucepan with 4 tbsp heavy cream and 1 tbsp sugar. Heat very gently until the chocolate has melted and the mixture is smooth.

"Perhaps it would be more useful if I were to transfigure Mr. Potter and yourself into a pocket watch?"

—PROFESSOR McGONAGALL
HARRY POTTER AND THE SORCERER'S STONE

HAGRID'S DRAGON EGGS

🍽 SERVES 6   ⏰ 45 MINS, PLUS COOLING   🔥 10 MINS

The more dangerous the magical creature, the fonder Hagrid will undoubtedly be of it—and in the wizarding world they don't come more deadly than dragons. Inspired by Norbert, the Norwegian Ridgeback acquired and cared for by the larger-than-life Gamekeeper when it was still in its shell, these patterned eggs are so tasty one definitely won't be enough. We just hope for your sake a Hungarian Horntail doesn't pop out!

FOR THE EGGS

6 large eggs

4 black tea bags

Scant ½ cup/120 ml dark soy sauce

TO FINISH

Several handfuls of spinach leaves

1 cup/100 g Bombay snack mix, salted pretzels, or Twiglets

Thousand Island dressing, to serve

1. Put the eggs in a small saucepan in which they fit quite snugly. Slowly pour over freshly boiled water to cover. Cook for 5 minutes. Lift the eggs out of the water with a spoon and place in a bowl of cold water to cool quickly. Tap the eggs gently on the work surface, rotating them as you go until the eggs are cracked all over, not forgetting the tops and bases!

2. Add the tea bags to the saucepan and return to boil. Lift out the tea bags once the water is dark brown, squeezing out as much liquid as you can using a teaspoon against the side of the pan. Add the soy sauce to the pan and carefully lower in the eggs. Cook for an additional 5 minutes and leave the eggs to cool completely in the liquid.

3. Carefully peel away the shells from the eggs to reveal the marbled whites. Scatter the spinach leaves onto a large plate and place the eggs in the center. Scatter the snack mix around the eggs to resemble a nest. Serve with the dressing.

TOP TIP

Thousand Island dressing is very easy to make. Simply beat together ⅓ cup/75 g mayonnaise in a bowl with 2 tsp tomato puree or ketchup, ¼ tsp mild chili powder, and a squeeze of lemon juice.

MAGICAL FACT

Norbert the baby Norwegian Ridgeback was entirely computer generated by the clever visual effects team on *Harry Potter and the Sorcerer's Stone*.

THE BOY WHO LIVED TOASTIES

 MAKES 1   **10 MINS**   **5 MINS**

Lightning bolt scar. Check. Glasses. Check. Unruly hair. Check. This fun and easy-to-follow recipe shows you how to re-create Harry Potter's famous features . . . in sandwich form. We've recommended ham and cheese for the filling as the combination is simply delicious, but cheese with shredded onion is just as tasty. And the eggplant glasses provide a welcome veggie boost.

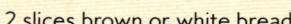

2 slices brown or white bread

A little butter for spreading and frying

2 slices of ham

2–3 cheddar cheese slices

2 very thin slices eggplant/aubergine, each about 1½ inches/4 cm in diameter

4 tbsp barbecue sauce

SPECIAL EQUIPMENT
1¼ inch/3 cm cookie cutter
Small plastic or paper piping bag

1   Butter the bread and sandwich with the ham and one of the cheese slices.

2   Heat a dot of butter in a small frying pan and fry the eggplant slices for a couple of minutes on each side to soften. Slide out of the pan onto a board and cut out the center using a 1¼ inch/3 cm cookie cutter. Add the sandwich to the pan and cook for 1 minute to toast the base.

3   Preheat your oven's grill or broiler to high. Arrange the remaining cheese slices to cover the sandwich and briefly grill to melt the cheese. Arrange the two eggplant circles on the sandwich.

4   Spoon the barbecue sauce into a small plastic or paper piping bag and snip off the tip. Use it to pipe the bridge of the glasses and Harry's scar. Use the remaining sauce to pipe hair.

MAGICAL FACT

Over the course of the eight movies, Harry's famous scar was applied to actor Daniel Radcliffe's forehead around 5,800 times. Wow!

MUNCHY OWL MAIL

 MAKES 6 **I HOUR** **35 MINS**

Wizarding post is a little bit different from Muggle mail, as Harry discovers with delight when an owl delivers his first-ever letter to 4 Privet Drive (only for Mr. Dursley to thwart him before he can read it). Designed in the shape of envelopes, these delicious chorizo and pepper-filled treats will be just as eagerly received by your family and friends. If you don't fancy making your own crepes, large, plain tortillas can be used instead.

FOR THE CREPES

I cup/125 g all-purpose/plain flour

I large egg

1¹/₃ cups/340 ml milk

Vegetable oil for frying

FOR THE FILLING

2 red peppers

I tbsp vegetable oil

I large red onion, diced

I cup/120 g finely diced chorizo

¼ cup/75 g ready-made thick tomato sauce

¼ cup/75 g red pepper, tomato, sweet corn, or onion relish

TO FINISH

Edible black cake pen

SPECIAL EQUIPMENT

Small round metal cutter, about I inch/2.5 cm in diameter

1 To make the crepes, put the flour in a large bowl and make a dip in the center. Break in the egg and a little of the milk. Use a whisk to beat together the egg and milk, gradually working in the flour. Slowly pour in the remaining milk, whisking until the batter is completely smooth.

2 Heat a little oil in a frying pan until it is very hot, tilting the pan so the oil coats the base. Add a ladleful of the batter and tilt the pan so the batter fills the base. Cook for about I minute until the crepe is golden on the underside. Use a spatula to flip the crepe over and very briefly cook the base. Slide the crepe out of the pan onto a large plate. Make five more crepes in the same way, adding a little more oil to the pan each time.

3 For the filling, stamp out three small circles from one pepper using the cutter and reserve for decoration. Dice the remaining peppers. Heat the oil in the pan and gently fry the onion, peppers, and chorizo for 8 minutes, stirring frequently. Stir in the tomato sauce and relish and remove from the heat.

Continues on page 78

> "Dad, look, Harry's got a letter!"
>
> —DUDLEY DURSLEY
> *Harry Potter and the Sorcerer's Stone*

TOP TIP

Instead of whisking the crepe mixture in a bowl, you can put all the ingredients in a food processor and blend together until completely smooth.

How to fold your crepe envelope

#1 Fold   Fold

#2 Fold   Fold

#3

4 Preheat the oven to 400°F/200°C/gas mark 6. Line a baking sheet with parchment paper. Place the crepes on the work surface with the palest sides facedown. Spoon the filling into the center of each and flatten down slightly. Fold two opposite sides of the crepes over the filling so the sides almost meet. Press down gently. Fold the lower side up and the top side down to enclose the filling and make a shape that's roughly square. Transfer three squares to the baking sheet and position a red pepper circle on the center of each.

5 Turn the remaining three crepes over and write Harry's address using the cake pen. Add these to the baking sheet. Bake the crepes for 12 minutes and serve hot.

TOP TIP

You can make these crepes several hours ahead of eating. Assemble and decorate, then chill on the baking sheet so they're ready to pop in the oven before serving.

Harry's address
(in case you need a little reminder)

MR. H. POTTER.
The Cupboard under the Stairs.
4, Privet Drive,
Little Whinging,
SURREY

MAGICAL FACT

For the scene in which hundreds of letters fly around the Dursleys' living room, the production team printed more than 10,000 envelopes with Harry's address on them. The envelopes were especially light so they could be blown about with ease.

GIANT CAULDRON SANDWICH

SERVES 4–6   **45 MINS**   **2 MINS**

As well as robes and course books, first-year Hogwarts students must purchase a cauldron, which they use to brew potions—often with explosive, house points-deducting results. This cauldron-inspired lunchtime treat, by comparison, is anything but a disaster. From ham and lettuce to avocado and cucumber, it contains layer after layer of delicious sandwich ingredients, which are revealed one by one when it's sliced. Yum!

I small round loaf, about 7 inches/18 cm diameter

Softened butter, for spreading

8–10 slices ham

¼ cucumber, thinly sliced

I large avocado, thinly sliced

4–6 tbsp tomato salsa

Several outer lettuce leaves

TO DECORATE

¼ cup/45 g corn/sweetcorn

3 large carrots

1   Holding a bread knife horizontally, cut a thin slice off the top of the loaf. Use a large metal spoon to scoop out as much of the soft center of the bread as possible to leave a thin crusty shell. Try to keep as much of the center of the bread in one piece as you can so you can cut a slice from it later on. Spread the inside of the bread case with butter. You might find it easier to spread with the back of a spoon.

2   Layer a third of the ham slices on the base of the bread. Cover with half the cucumber and avocado, then spread with half the salsa. Arrange half the lettuce leaves on top, then half the remaining ham.

3   Cut a slice of the scooped-out bread as best you can. (You might need to make a patchwork of pieces.) Butter the underside, place over the ham, then butter the top. Layer up the remaining ingredients into the bread, finishing with a layer of ham. Wrap and chill until ready to serve.

4   To decorate your sandwich, cook the corn in boiling water for 2 minutes, then drain. Using a potato peeler, shave as many ribbons of carrot as you can. Pile up on a large serving plate and spread them out in a thick layer. You can reserve some of the ribbons and cut the ends to look like flames. Position the bread and arrange the cut ribbons so they lick the sides of the cauldron. Scatter the corn over the top layer of ham and serve.

TOP TIP

The amount of filling you can pack into the bread depends on the width and depth of your loaf, so you might need a little extra or a little less. If you have any other favorite sandwich fillings, use them instead, as long as they're not too wet!

"FLUFFY" BAKED POTATOES

 SERVES 3   30 MINS   🔲 1¼ HOUR

This inventive recipe shows you how to create your own version of Fluffy, the enormous, three-headed dog whose bite is most definitely worse than its bark—just ask Professor Snape, who got on the wrong side of the beast in *Harry Potter and the Sorcerer's Stone*. With radish fangs and claws, these tasty and very healthy baked potatoes may look a little scary, but just play some soothing music while eating and you'll be fine.

 V **GF**

3 similar-sized baking potatoes

2 tbsp olive oil

Good pinch of salt

4 small potatoes

2 long strips of eggplant/aubergine skin

Handful of radishes

3 tbsp gluten-free barbecue sauce

6 capers

3 small pieces of black olive

SPECIAL EQUIPMENT
Small paper or plastic piping bag

1 Preheat the oven to 400°F/200°C/gas mark 6. Place the baking potatoes in a roasting tin and brush with most of the oil. Sprinkle with salt and bake for 30 minutes. Add the small potatoes to the tin, brush with the remaining oil, and bake for an additional 20 minutes. Finally, add the eggplant to the tin and bake for another 10 minutes or until all the potatoes are very soft when pierced with a knife. Leave until cool enough to handle.

2 Transfer the large potatoes to a board. Use your hands (wrapped in a tea towel if the potatoes are still hot) to push down the potatoes at one end to create a snout shape. Arrange the potatoes in a shallow ovenproof serving dish, tucking the small potatoes in place for the paws.

3 Cut six triangular shapes from the eggplant for ears. Make two slits on top of each potato and push the pieces in place. Cut thin slices of radish and cut out oval shapes for eyes. Cut fangs from radish slices and little claws from the radish skin. Make further slits near the bases of the potatoes and push in the fangs, then position the claws.

4 Put the barbecue sauce in a small paper or plastic piping bag and snip off the tip so the sauce can be piped in a fine line. Use dots of the sauce to secure the eyes in place, then add capers for the centers of the eyes. Use more of the sauce to secure the black olive nose. Finally, decorate the eyes and the paws with piped sauce.

5 Return the potatoes, on the ovenproof dish, to the oven for 5-10 minutes to heat through before serving.

MAGICAL FACT

Fluffy has one weakness: the sound of music. It sends him straight to sleep!

TOP TIP
★ ★
Baking potatoes have a soft texture, sometimes described as "floury," so they're nice and "fluffy" to eat. Small potatoes are usually firmer and sometimes called "waxy." You'll notice the different textures when you cut into them.

DESSERTS & TREATS

"Baked it myself, words and all!"

RUBEUS HAGRID

If you're in possession of a sweet tooth, then
you're going to especially enjoy this section.
It's full to bursting with sugary goodness . . .
a bit like Honeydukes Sweet Shop, in fact!

"IMMOBULUS" PUDDING

 SERVES 8-10 **45 MINUTES, PLUS FREEZING** **3-5 MINS**

With a whipped meringue topping that goes here, there, and everywhere, this fun pudding looks like it's been stopped in its tracks—a bit like the naughty Cornish pixies in *Harry Potter and the Chamber of Secrets* when Hermione casts the Freezing Charm, *Immobulus*. The sponge, fruit, and vanilla ice cream at its center will also bring you to a halt . . . but only because it's so delicious.

I homemade or bought sponge cake or roll, about 12 oz/350 g

4 tbsp raspberry or strawberry jam

1¾ pints/1 liter vanilla ice cream

1½ cups/180 g fresh or frozen raspberries, halved

4 large egg whites

1⅛ cup/225 g granulated sugar

SPECIAL EQUIPMENT

Shallow ovenproof dish or tin, about 10 inches/25 cm in diameter

Ice cream scoop, optional

TOP TIP

This pudding is similar to a very retro recipe called Baked Alaska. You can mix and match the flavors by using different sponge bases such as chocolate, coffee, or coconut. The ice cream can be any of your favorite flavors. The secret is to make sure that the ice cream is very solid before covering with the meringue and baking.

1 First, make sure you have enough space in your freezer to fit a 10 inch/25 cm round shallow ovenproof dish or tin that will be piled high with filling. Roughly slice the cake and pack into the base of the dish. Spread with the jam.

2 Use a tablespoon or ice cream scoop to pile a little of the ice cream on top, dotting raspberries in and around the ice cream. Continue to layer up the ice cream and fruit. This doesn't have to be neat, as long as you make a shape that's domed up in the center. Transfer to the freezer until step 4.

3 Put the egg whites in a large, thoroughly clean bowl and whisk with a handheld electric whisk until peaking. Add a tablespoonful of the sugar and whisk again for 10 seconds. Add another spoonful of the sugar. Continue to whisk the mixture, gradually adding the remaining sugar in the same way, until the meringue is thick and glossy.

4 Scrape the meringue out onto the ice cream and spread it in an even layer until the pudding is completely covered. Make sure there are no thin areas of meringue with the ice cream showing through. Use the back of a spoon to create peaks all over the meringue. Return the pudding to the freezer for at least 1 hour.

5 To serve, transfer the pudding to the fridge for about an hour. Preheat the oven to 475°F/240°C/gas mark 9. Lower the oven shelf if necessary so there's plenty of room for the meringue. Transfer the pudding to the oven and bake for 3-5 minutes until the meringue peaks are deep golden. You'll need to watch closely as the meringue will very quickly overcook! Serve immediately.

DUMBLEDORE'S MYSTICAL LEMON DROP PUDDING

 SERVES 6   **25 MINS**   🔥 **30 MINS**

A well-known lover of sweets, with his absolute favorites being zingy lemon drops, Hogwarts headmaster Albus Dumbledore would definitely give his wizarding seal of approval to this amazingly clever baked pudding. It's a whisked, lemony-flavored mixture that separates during baking to produce a sweet spongy topping and a saucy layer underneath. Just like magic, in fact!

2 large lemons

1 cup/200 g granulated sugar

½ stick/55 g butter, softened

⅔ cup/85 g all-purpose/plain flour

3 large eggs, separated

1⅓ cups/340 ml milk

Confectioners'/icing sugar, for dusting

1 Preheat the oven to 350°F/180°C/gas mark 4. Use a fine grater to grate the outer part of the skin, the "zest", from the lemons. Halve the lemons and squeeze the juice. There should be a generous ⅓ cup/80 ml. Put the sugar, butter, flour, lemon zest, and egg yolks in a bowl with a little of the milk and beat with a whisk until pale and creamy. Gradually beat in the remaining milk and the lemon juice until combined. Don't worry if the mixture starts to look a little curdled at this stage!

2 Put the egg whites in a thoroughly clean bowl and whisk until the mixture forms soft peaks when the whisk is lifted from the bowl. Scrape the egg whites into the lemon mixture. Using a large metal spoon, fold the egg whites into the sauce until the mixture is combined (see Top Tip).

3 Turn into a shallow ovenproof dish and stand the dish in a roasting tin. Pour a ¾ inch/2 cm depth of very hot water into the tin. Carefully transfer to the oven and bake for 30 minutes until the pudding has risen and the crust is golden. The surface should feel a little wobbly when gently pressed with your fingers. Serve warm, dusted with confectioners' sugar.

TOP TIP

When adding whisked egg whites to a batter, the ingredients are "folded" rather than stirred together so you don't lose all the airiness of the whites. Using a large metal spoon, scoop up the batter from under the whites and turn it up and over the egg whites. Repeat this process in another part of the bowl so the whites and batter are gradually blended together. Keep doing this until there are no lumps of egg whites in the mixture.

MAGICAL FACT

As well as lemon drops, Albus Dumbledore is also fond of licorice snaps, a magical sweet with a sharp bite . . . literally, as Harry discovers!

Devil's Snare Apple Pie

 **SERVES 8** **1 HOUR, PLUS CHILLLING** **50 MINS**

This large, fruity pie definitely wouldn't look out of place at a Hogwarts feast, although Harry, Ron, and Hermione might think twice about eating it, as the long, twisted tendrils of pastry on top are shaped to resemble Devil's Snare, the dangerous plant that tightens its grip the more you wriggle. Thankfully, this version is completely harmless. The only thing it'll ensnare, in fact, is your taste buds!

FOR THE PASTRY

2¾ cups/345 g all-purpose/plain flour

Good pinch of salt

1 cup/225 g unsalted butter, firm, diced

⅛ cup/25 g granulated sugar

2 egg yolks

1 tbsp cold water

FOR THE FILLING

2¼ lb/1 kg cooking apples, peeled and cored

½ cup/100 g granulated sugar

½ tsp ground cinnamon, optional

½ stick/55 g unsalted butter, diced

1 egg, to glaze

Natural brown food coloring

SPECIAL EQUIPMENT

Food processor (see Top Tip)

Approximately 9½ inch/24 cm shallow ovenproof or metal pie plate

1. To make the pastry, put the flour, salt, and butter in a food processor and blend until the mixture resembles bread crumbs. Add the sugar, egg yolks, and 1 tbsp cold water and blend again until the mixture forms a dough. Wrap and chill for 30 minutes.

2. Slice the apples and place in a large bowl of cold water. This will stop the apple slices from turning brown. Combine the sugar and cinnamon (if using) in a separate bowl.

3. Cut the pastry dough in half. Dust the work surface with flour and roll out half the pastry to a circle measuring at least 11 inches/28 cm in diameter. Carefully lift the pastry into the pie plate and press it gently to fit up the sides and over the rim. Trim off the excess pastry with a knife.

4. Drain the apple slices and arrange half in the plate. Sprinkle with half the cinnamon sugar and dot with half the butter. Pile the remaining apples on top, then add the remaining sugar and butter.

5. Beat the egg in a small bowl with a few drops of brown food coloring. Brush the rim of the pastry with a little beaten egg.

6. Roll out the remaining pastry and cut with a knife into irregular-width strips, measuring between ½ inch/1 cm wide and ¼ inch/0.5 cm wide. Use your fingers to pinch the strips into more rounded shapes and lay them over the filling, bending and twisting the lengths together to look snare-like. Re-roll the pastry trimmings under the palms of your hands into lengths of different thicknesses and arrange over the pie in the same way until the filling is almost completely covered. Chill for 30 minutes.

7. Preheat the oven to 400°F/200°C/gas mark 6. Place a baking sheet onto the oven shelf. Brush the pastry with the beaten egg, place on the baking sheet, and bake for 50 minutes until deep golden. Serve warm with cream, custard, or vanilla ice cream.

HOGWARTS EXPRESS GINGERBREAD COOKIES

 MAKES ABOUT 10   **1-1½ HOURS, PLUS CHILLING**   **15-20 MINS**

The journey from Platform 9¾ in London to Hogsmeade Station in the far north is a long one, so it's best to ensure you're loaded with delicious snacks. As well as Bertie Bott's Every Flavor Beans, Chocolate Frogs, and crumpled sandwiches (made with love by Mrs. Weasley), we recommend these delicious gingerbread cookies. With 10 in a batch, meaning plenty to go around, they're not just great for trains, but plane, car, and ferry trips too!

FOR THE GINGERBREAD DOUGH

- ¾ stick/85 g butter, cut into small dice
- ⅓ cup/75 g light brown sugar
- 2 egg yolks
- 4 tbsp corn syrup/golden syrup
- 1½ cups/190 g all-purpose/plain flour
- ¼ tsp baking powder
- 1 tbsp ground ginger

TO DECORATE

- 3½ oz/100 g red fondant
- Confectioners'/icing sugar for dusting
- Tube of white decorator frosting/icing
- Several soft licorice sticks or ribbons
- Handful of small round colored candies/sweets
- Approximately 10 white jelly beans
- Edible red or black cake pen

SPECIAL EQUIPMENT
Food processor

1 To make the gingerbread, put all the dough ingredients into a food processor and blend until the mixture comes together to form a dough. Tip out onto the surface, wrap in plastic wrap, and chill for 30 minutes.

2 Preheat the oven to 350°F/180°C/gas mark 4. Line a baking sheet with parchment paper. Trace and cut out the train template on page 120. Turn the dough out onto a lightly floured surface and roll out to a scant ¼ inch/5 mm thickness. Place the template over the dough and cut out the train shape using a small sharp knife. Transfer to the baking sheet and cut out as many more trains as you can from the pastry. (You can also re-roll the trimmings to make more.) Chill on the baking sheet for 20 minutes.

3 Bake the cookies for 15-20 minutes until they begin to brown around the edges. Leave on the baking sheet for 5 minutes, then transfer to a wire rack to cool.

Continues on page 94

4 Trace and cut out the red plate template on page 120. Thinly roll out the red fondant on a surface lightly dusted with confectioners' sugar. Lay the template on top and cut around it with a small sharp knife. Squeeze a little decorator frosting at the top of a train cookie (this will act as glue), and position the red fondant. Cut out a 3 x ½ inch/7.5 x 1 cm rectangle and secure along the base of the train in the same way. Cut out and position more shapes on the remaining cookies. Secure thin strips of red fondant trimmings around the funnels.

5 Using a small sharp knife, cut the licorice into thin strips and position next to the red fondant. Cut smaller pieces to cover the wheels. Again, use the decorator frosting to secure in place.

6 Pipe "5972" onto the front of the cookies and then secure the colored candies and jelly beans in place using more decorator frosting. Use the cake pen to draw the Hogwarts crest onto the jelly beans.

MAGICAL FACT

The Hogwarts Express is made of real steam train parts: the locomotive "5972 Olton Hall" and four (later five) British Railways Mark I passenger carriages.

"LEVICORPUS" UPSIDE-DOWN CAKE

🍽️ SERVES 8   🕐 30 MINS   🔲 40 MINS

This scrumptious dessert is entirely the wrong way up—just like the end result of *Levicorpus*, a jinx where the victim is left hanging upside down. The pineapple and cherries are arranged in the base of a cake tin, then topped with sponge mixture. After baking, the dish is inverted onto a serving plate to reveal a beautiful layer of fruit. A recipe so delicious it'll definitely leave you feeling topsy-turvy. Serve as it comes or with cream or ice cream.

V **GF**

6-7 canned pineapple slices, drained

Several fresh, candied, or glacé
   cherries

¾ cup/180 g unsalted butter, softened

¾ cup/170 g light brown sugar

Zest and juice of 1 lime

2 large eggs

⅔ cup/125 g polenta

1 tsp gluten-free baking powder

1¼ cups/125 g ground almonds

TO FINISH

⅓ cup/70 g granulated sugar

4 tbsp water

Juice of 2 limes

Edible gold glitter stars

SPECIAL EQUIPMENT
8 inch/20 cm round cake tin

1   Preheat the oven to 350°F/180°C/gas mark 4. Grease an 8 inch/20 cm round cake tin and line the base with a circle of parchment paper. Halve the pineapple slices and cherries. Arrange the pineapple slices in the tin, leaving a small gap in between the pieces so they're not touching. Fill the bigger spaces with cherries, cut sides faceup.

2   Beat together the butter, sugar, and lime zest in a bowl until pale and creamy. Gradually beat in the eggs. Add the polenta, baking powder, and almonds and mix well. Spoon the mixture into the tin, spreading it carefully so you don't dislodge the fruit.

3   Level the surface with the back of a spoon and bake for about 40 minutes until risen and golden. The surface should feel firm and a skewer inserted into the center should come out clean.

4   While the mixture is baking, make a syrup. Put the sugar in a small saucepan with 4 tbsp water and heat very gently until the sugar dissolves. Bring to a boil and boil for 3-4 minutes until turning syrupy. Remove from the heat and stir in the lime juice.

5   Loosen the edges of the cake by running a knife between the cake and the tin. Rest a serving plate on top. Holding both plate and tin firmly, flip them over and lift away the tin. Peel away the parchment and spoon the syrup over. Just before serving, sprinkle with a swirl of glitter stars.

TOP TIP
⭐ ⭐

Polenta and ground almonds are used in this cake instead of regular flour. If you want to ensure that the cake is completely gluten-free, make sure the baking powder is gluten-free too.

MAGICAL FACT

Levicorpus, also known as the Dangling Jinx, was invented by the Half-Blood Prince (aka Severus Snape) when he was a student at Hogwarts.

CORNELIUS FUDGE'S FUDGE

 MAKES 25-30 **20 MINS, PLUS CHILLING**

This flavorsome fudge is great for chefs young and old alike, as it's incredibly easy to make. It uses just three ingredients, plus a tint of green food coloring to illustrate the floo flames that carry witches and wizards in and out of the Ministry of Magic—the scene of a fearsome climatic battle in *Harry Potter and the Order of the Phoenix*. Sweet and creamy, this is definitely a special occasion treat rather than an everyday nibble!

 V **GF**

¼ cup/60 g coconut oil

2 cups/300 g white chocolate chips or chopped chocolate

½ cup/100 ml heavy/double cream

Natural green food coloring

SPECIAL EQUIPMENT
6 inch/18 cm square metal or plastic container

1 Line a square 6 inch/18 cm metal or plastic container with a sheet of parchment paper, pushing the paper into the corners. Put the coconut oil and chocolate in a heatproof bowl and rest the bowl over a pan of gently simmering water, making sure that the base of the bowl is not in contact with the water. Turn off the heat and leave the mixture until melted and smooth, stirring gently once or twice.

2 Whip the cream in a bowl with a dash of green food coloring. Add the melted chocolate mixture and stir gently to mix. Scrape into the container and spread level. Chill for several hours or overnight.

3 Lift out of the container and peel away the paper. Cut into small squares to serve. The fudge is quite soft so if the knife gets messy you might need to clean it after several cuts. Store uneaten fudge in the fridge.

> "Come now, Harry, the Ministry doesn't send people to Azkaban for blowing up their aunts."
>
> —CORNELIUS FUDGE
> *HARRY POTTER AND THE PRISONER OF AZKABAN*

MAGICAL FACT

Cornelius Fudge became Minister of Magic in 1990. It is rumored he only got the job because Albus Dumbledore turned it down.

Aragog Muffins

 **MAKES 12**  **1 HOUR, PLUS COOLING** 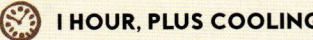 **20 MINS**

A good deal cuter than the real Aragog—whose piercing eyes and eight enormous legs have Ron whimpering with fright in the second film—these yummy spidery snacks will be devoured by your guests in no time. Although equally delicious, muffins don't store as well as sponge cakes, so it's best to make them on the day you serve them, or make ahead and freeze.

FOR THE MUFFINS

2 cups/250 g all-purpose/plain flour

1 tbsp baking powder

¼ cup/30 g cocoa powder

¾ cup/170 g light brown sugar

¾ cup/175 ml milk

2 large eggs, beaten

⅓ cup/80 ml light olive oil or vegetable oil

½ cup/75 g milk chocolate chips, or chopped chocolate

TO DECORATE

½ stick/55 g butter, softened

⅔ cup/85 g confectioners'/icing sugar

2 tbsp cocoa powder

1 tsp boiling water

9 soft black round candies/sweets, about ¾ inch/2 cm in diameter

Several licorice ropes or wheels

18 white baker's edible eyes

Tube of white decorator frosting/icing

> **SPECIAL EQUIPMENT**
> 12-section muffin tray
> 12 paper liners, preferably black
> Palette knife

1 Preheat the oven to 375°F/190°C/gas mark 5. Line a 12-section muffin tray with paper liners. Sift the flour, baking powder, and cocoa powder into a large bowl. Stir in the sugar.

2 Add the milk, eggs, oil, and chocolate and stir the ingredients together until just mixed. There should be a few specks of the dry ingredients still visible. Spoon the mixture into the paper liners and bake for 20 minutes or until risen and just firm to the touch. Transfer to a wire rack and leave to cool completely.

3 To decorate, put the butter, sugar, cocoa powder, and 1 tsp boiling water in a bowl and beat for a couple of minutes until the mixture is smooth and creamy. Spoon a little onto each muffin and spread almost to the edges with a palette knife.

4 Place a black round candy in the center of nine of the muffins. Cut the licorice ropes into ¾ inch/2 cm lengths. If using a licorice wheel, unroll it, cut across into ¾ inch/2 cm lengths, and cut each length in half. Bend and arrange four licorice pieces on the side of each candy for spider legs, pushing them down into the frosting to secure. Secure two baker's edible eyes to each spider, securing in place with dots of decorator frosting.

5 Use the decorator frosting to pipe spiderwebs onto the remaining three muffins.

DRACO MALFOY BLONDIES

 MAKES 20 **20 MINS** **25 MINS**

Named for their pale exterior, these easy-to-make blondies are actually everything that Harry's archenemy Draco Malfoy isn't: sweet, well-presented, and undeniably good. They take just 25 minutes to bake, so you'll be tempted to eat them straight out of the oven (once they've cooled slightly, of course), but it's best to wait a while before digging in, as they slice so much better when completely cold.

- $2\frac{2}{3}$ cups/400 g white chocolate chips or chopped chocolate
- ¼ cup/60 g butter
- 3 large eggs
- ½ cup/110 g granulated sugar
- $1\frac{1}{3}$ cups/170 g all-purpose/plain flour
- 1 tsp baking powder
- 1 cup/125 g chopped walnuts or pecan nuts

SPECIAL EQUIPMENT
11 x 9 inch/28 x 23 cm shallow rectangular baking tin

1. Preheat the oven to 375°F/190°C/gas mark 5. Take a large rectangle of parchment paper and fit it into an 11 x 9 inch/28 x 23 cm shallow rectangular baking tin. Crease the paper into the corners of the tin.

2. Reserve half the chocolate. Put the remainder in a heatproof bowl with the butter. Place the bowl over a saucepan of gently simmering water, making sure that the base of the bowl is not in contact with the water. Leave until melted, stirring occasionally.

3. In a separate bowl, beat together the eggs and sugar with a handheld electric whisk for 4-5 minutes until the mixture is foamy. Scrape the melted chocolate mixture, remaining chocolate, flour, baking powder, and nuts into the bowl and stir until smooth.

4. Turn into the tin and spread the mixture into the corners. Bake for 25 minutes until risen and golden. Leave to cool completely in the tin before cutting into squares.

DID YOU KNOW?
Blondies are a white chocolate version of chocolate brownies, which originated in the United States over one hundred years ago.

MAGICAL FACT
One of Draco's most famous quotes in the Harry Potter films: "Reading? I didn't know you could read!" was improvised by actor Tom Felton when he forgot his line.

HEDWIG MERINGUES

  SERVES 8    I HOUR   50–60 MINS

Presented to Harry by Hagrid as a gift for his eleventh birthday, snowy owl Hedwig is a loyal and true friend to The Boy Who Lived, even if she does give him a nip now and then (usually when he's late visiting the Hogwarts Owlery). This recipe shows you how to make your own melt-in-the-mouth meringue versions of Harry's feathery animal companion. Trust us when we say that one won't be enough . . .

V   **GF**

FOR THE MERINGUES

3 large egg whites

¾ cup/150 g caster sugar

TO FINISH

4 raisins, cut in half

Handful of flaked almonds

Tubes of yellow and brown or black decorator frosting/icing

1 Preheat the oven to 250°F/130°C/gas mark ½. Line a large baking sheet with parchment paper.

2 Whisk the egg whites in a thoroughly clean bowl until just peaking. Add a tablespoon of the sugar and whisk again for 10 seconds. Add another tablespoon of the sugar. Continue to whisk the mixture, gradually adding the remaining sugar in the same way, until the meringue is thick and glossy.

3 Spoon a heaped tablespoonful (an eighth of the mixture) onto the baking sheet. Use a second spoon to release it from the first. Spread with the back of a spoon to a shape that measures 3 x 2½ inches/7.5 x 6 cm. Use the back of a teaspoon to make two deep craters for the eye sockets.

4 Position a raisin halfway between the eyes for the beak. Push plenty of flaked almonds into the meringue for feathers. Bake for about 50–60 minutes until the meringue feels just crisp when tapped. If necessary bake a little longer. Leave to cool.

5 Decorate the eyes by piping large circles of yellow frosting and small centers of brown or black frosting.

MAGICAL FACT

Despite being a female owl in the story, Hedwig was portrayed onscreen by several male snowy owls, with one owl in particular—a fantastic beast named Gizmo—being used for most of the scenes.

TOP TIP

The secret to perfect meringues is to give the mixture a good whisk in between each addition of sugar. If the sugar is added too quickly, the egg whites won't be able to hold it and syrup will seep out of the meringues during baking.

ROOM OF REQUIRE-MINTS

MAKES ABOUT 18   **20 MINS**

Located on the seventh floor of Hogwarts castle, the Room of Requirement is a truly wondrous place, appearing only to those in great need of it. Should you ever be "in need" of minty morsels so fresh and zingy that they'll clear your head in seconds, then this is the recipe for you. What's more, they're so easy to make and "require" very few ingredients.

1 egg white

2 cups/250 g confectioners'/icing sugar

1 cup/75 g desiccated coconut

1 tsp mint extract

¼ cup/40 g milk chocolate chips or chopped chocolate

1 Use a fork to whisk the egg white until it's completely broken up but still liquid. Put the sugar, coconut, and mint extract in a bowl and add a generous tablespoon of the egg white. Mix the ingredients well until they cling together. Use your hands to pack the ingredients into a firm paste. If still very crumbly, add a dash more egg white, but don't add too much or the mixture will be too sticky.

2 Turn the paste onto the surface and form into a thin log shape about 9 inches/23 cm long. Use a sharp knife to cut the log across into ½ inch/1 cm thick slices. Place on a sheet of parchment paper.

3 Place the chocolate in a heatproof bowl and stand it over a pan of simmering water. Turn off the heat and leave the chocolate until melted and smooth. Use a teaspoon to drizzle the chocolate over the mints. Leave to cool. Once the mints are cool, they can be stacked in a jar or box and stored in a cool place for several days.

MAGICAL FACT

Instead of cushions (as described in the book), production designer Stuart Craig decided to fill the Room of Requirement with mirrors. "Photographically, the reflections offered exciting possibilities," he explained.

DRINKS

"Three Butterbeers and some ginger in mine, please!"

— HERMIONE GRANGER —

These fresh and fruity drinks—all with
a magical twist—will go down a treat
with children and adults alike. Just watch
out for that Grindylow!

HOGWARTS HOUSES SMOOTHIE

 MAKES 2 SMALL GLASSES **20 MINS**

Impress your friends with this refreshing drink that represents the four Hogwarts houses. The trick is to build up the layers as carefully as you can so that the different-colored fruits remain separate. Start with kiwi at the bottom (green for Slytherin), then top with blueberries (blue for Ravenclaw). Next add the pineapple (yellow for Hufflepuff) and finally the strawberries (red for Gryffindor). Or mix them up if you'd prefer!

 V VG GF

1/3 small pineapple, skinned

1 cup/175 g strawberries

2 kiwi fruit, skinned

1 cup/125 g blueberries

SPECIAL EQUIPMENT

Small blender or food processor

TOP TIP

Some fruits are thicker than others when blended. If very thick, add just a dash of water to thin, but don't add too much or you won't be able to layer the colors.

1 Roughly chop the pineapple, discarding the core, and puree in a small blender or food processor until completely smooth. Pineapple has a dense texture, so you might need to add a little water so it's not too thick. Transfer to a small bowl.

2 Blend the remaining fruit in the same way, rinsing out the blender in between each and placing the purees in separate bowls.

3 Spoon one fruit into two glasses, taking care that the juice doesn't spill on the sides. Stop filling the glasses once about a quarter full. Lower another spoonful of a different fruit on top. Avoid pouring or spooning from higher than the rim of the glasses or the colors will merge. Repeat with the remaining fruit and serve, or chill until ready to serve.

GRYFFINDOR

HUFFLEPUFF

RAVENCLAW

SLYTHERIN

TOP TIP
⭐

Despite the name, blueberries turn a pinky/purple color when blended, so add a little natural blue food coloring if you want a truer Ravenclaw blue!

TOP TIP

★

Small amounts of any leftover vegetables such as broccoli florets, chopped asparagus, pepper, or French beans can be used in this recipe instead of those suggested on the right—just as long as they're green!

Troll Bogey Delight

  MAKES I GLASS · **10 MINS**

"Errr, troll bogeys . . ." The name of this drink might have you wrinkling up your nose in the same way Harry did after his close encounter with a troll in *Harry Potter and the Sorcerer's Stone*, but the flavor couldn't be tastier! It's also a good way of getting green vegetables, such as kale and cucumber, into your diet if you wouldn't normally like to see them on your dinner plate.

Small handful torn kale leaves

½ avocado, seed and skin removed

I inch/2.5 cm piece cucumber, diced

Good squeeze of lemon or lime juice

I tsp clear honey

I cup/250 ml green grape, pear, or apple juice

½ passion fruit

SPECIAL EQUIPMENT
Blender or food processor

1. Place all the ingredients except the passion fruit into a blender or food processor and blend until completely smooth, scraping down any pieces that cling to the side.

2. Pour into a glass and scoop the passion fruit onto the surface of the smoothie using a teaspoon.

MAGICAL FACT

The troll Hermione, Ron, and Harry bravely defeat in the girls' bathroom in *Harry Potter and the Sorcerer's Stone* is a mountain troll, and a 12-foot one at that! The encounter results in Hermione getting five points deducted from Gryffindor, while Ron and Harry are awarded five points each.

"TROLL . . . in the dungeon! Troll in the dungeon! I thought you ought to know."

—PROFESSOR QUIRRELL
HARRY POTTER AND THE SORCERER'S STONE

Pumpkin Patch Surprise

 **MAKES 2 GLASSES** **20 MINS** **10 MINS**

Inspired by pumpkin juice—a popular drink in the wizarding world, especially on all-important occasions such as Halloween—this delicious recipe is rather like drinking the flavors of a festive pumpkin pie. It's stupendously spicy (especially if you're brave enough to add the pepper sauce) and the perfect treat (or some might say trick) for your All Hallows' Eve—or any other—party. When fresh pumpkin is not available, use canned (see Top Tip).

V **GF**

- 2½ cups/500 g diced fresh pumpkin (about ½ small pumpkin), seeds and skin removed
- ½ tsp pumpkin pie spice/ground mixed spice
- Juice of 1 lime
- 2–3 tbsp maple syrup, to taste
- ⅔ cup/150 ml milk (or any dairy-free milk)
- Ice cubes
- Tabasco, or other hot pepper sauce, to serve, optional

SPECIAL EQUIPMENT
Blender or food processor

1 Put the diced pumpkin and spice in a saucepan, just cover with water, and heat until simmering. Cook gently for 10 minutes until the pumpkin is tender. Drain through a sieve and leave to cool a little.

2 Transfer to a food processor or blender and add the lime juice, 2 tbsp of the maple syrup, and milk. Blend until completely smooth. Taste for sweetness, adding a little more maple syrup if you like.

3 Pour into two glasses, add several ice cubes to each, and sprinkle with pepper sauce if you like very spicy flavors.

TOP TIP

If only canned pumpkin puree is available, allow 1½ cups/350 g. Add a little extra milk once you've blended the juice if the consistency is too thick.

GRINDYLOW GULP

 MAKES 1 GLASS   20 MINS

A word of warning! Much like the Great Lake at Hogwarts, in which all manner of curious creatures dwell, a little water demon lurks in the depths of this tangy fruit juice. But don't worry, it's only a piece of canned pear, carved out to resemble a Grindylow's head. It's probably best to drink the juice and then eat the fruit with a spoon . . . if you dare!

2 tbsp granulated sugar

Dark green natural food coloring

½ canned pear

2 pumpkin seeds

Squeeze of lime juice

Approximately 1¼ cups/310 ml clear apple or pear juice

1 Put the sugar in a shallow bowl and add 2–3 drops of green food coloring. Use the back of a teaspoon to blend the color into the sugar until the sugar is evenly colored. You might find it easier to use your fingers once the color is nearly distributed. Dampen the rim of a glass with water and invert it into the sugar until the rim is coated.

2 Use the tip of a small sharp knife to trim away the pointed top of the pear half. Use the knife to cut out a long, curved mouth from near the base of the pear and through to the cored center. If you feel confident with the knife, cut out tiny teeth marks with the tip of the knife. Cut two more small cavities for eyes. These should be spaced well apart to look like a true Grindylow! Push the pumpkin seeds into the eye cavities.

3 Add a drop of green food coloring and a squeeze of lime to the fruit juice in a small jug. Stir to mix and pour into the sugared glass. Carefully lower the pear into the glass to serve.

MAGICAL FACT

Grindylows are creatures with sharp teeth who live in Hogwarts's Great Lake. To create the scene in *Harry Potter and the Goblet of Fire* where a horde of these frightening water demons grab at Harry, two stuntmen pulled at Daniel Radcliffe's legs in an underwater tank with a fitted green screen. The effects were added later.

TOP TIP

If you only have bright green food coloring, add the tiniest dash of brown or black food coloring along with the green to make the color slightly more murky!

TOP TIP
★
This tea is served hot. If you forget about it and it goes cold, it'll still taste good—you might even prefer it!

SyBill Trelawney's Divination Tea

 MAKES 2 GLASSES **5 MINS**

We don't need to sit through one of Professor Trelawney's dramatic Hogwarts Divination classes to predict that you're going to love this fresh and fruity drink. There are no tea leaves, but maybe you could have a go "reading" the orange shreds left at the bottom instead. Who knows, you may possess the "sight"! Just, whatever you do, don't spot a Grim . . .

V VG GF

I orange

2 tbsp maple syrup

2 strawberries, finely chopped

Several mint leaves, finely chopped

SPECIAL EQUIPMENT
Citrus zester, optional

1 Bring a half-filled kettle of water to a boil.

2 Zest and juice the orange and place in two glasses or mugs.

3 Add the maple syrup, strawberries, and mint leaves to the mugs and top up with boiling water. Stir well and serve.

TOP TIP
★ ★

If you don't have a citrus zester, use a coarse cheese grater instead.

> "Your aura is pulsing, dear. Are you in the beyond?"
>
> —Sybill Trelawney
> *Harry Potter and the Prisoner of Azkaban*

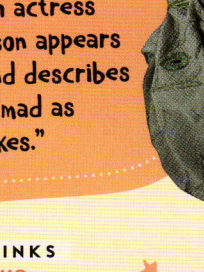

MAGICAL FACT

Professor Trelawney is played in the Harry Potter movies by Oscar-winning British actress Emma Thompson. Thompson appears in three films in total and describes her character as "mad as a bucket of snakes."

TEMPLATES

Trace these templates and cut them out to use on your bakes!

HOGWARTS TRUNK OF FOODIE FUN

MR. WEASLEY'S FLYING FORD ANGLIA

GOLDEN PEANUT SNITCHES

Cut along the dotted lines

HOGWARTS EXPRESS GINGERBREAD COOKIES

MEASUREMENT CONVERSION CHARTS

DRY WEIGHT

IMPERIAL	METRIC
½ oz	15 g
1 oz	29 g
2 oz	57 g
3 oz	85 g
4 oz	113 g
5 oz	141 g
6 oz	170 g
8 oz	227 g
10 oz	283 g
12 oz	340 g
14 oz	397 g
1 lb	453 g

LIQUID WEIGHT

CUPS	OZ	ML
1 tbsp	½ fl oz	15 ml
⅛ cup	1 fl oz	30 ml
¼ cup	2 fl oz	60 ml
⅓ cup	2½ fl oz	80 ml
½ cup	4 fl oz	120 ml
¾ cup	6 fl oz	175 ml
1 cup	8 fl oz	240 ml
1¼ cups	10 fl oz	300 ml
1½ cups	12 fl oz	355 ml
2 cups	16 fl oz	480 ml
2½ cups	21 fl oz	600 ml
3 cups	25 fl oz	725 ml

TEMPERATURE

FAHRENHEIT	CELSIUS
100°F	37°C
150°F	65°C
200°F	93°C
250°F	121°C
300°F	150°C
325°F	160°C
350°F	180°C
375°F	190°C
400°F	200°C
425°F	220°C
450°F	230°C
500°F	260°C

NOTE: All conversions are approximate.

Liquid Conversions

1 GALLON
4 quarts
8 pints
16 cups
128 fl oz
3.8 liters

1 QUART
2 pints
4 cups
32 fl oz
946 ml

1 PINT
2 cups
16 fl oz
480 ml

1 CUP
16 tbsp
8 fl oz
240 ml

¼ CUP
4 tbsp
2 fl oz
60 ml

1 tsp = 5ml

1 tbsp = 15ml

TOP TIP

When measuring using a cup, remember that dry ingredients should be leveled rather than piled up in the center of the cup.

If you measure wet ingredients first, rinse and dry the cup before measuring dry ingredients, otherwise the dry ingredients might stick to the cup.

INDEX

All rights reserved. Published by Scholastic Inc., *Publishers since 1920.*
SCHOLASTIC and associated logos are trademarks and/or registered trademarks of Scholastic Inc.

Scholastic Inc., 557 Broadway, New York, NY 10012

Scholastic UK Ltd., 1 London Bridge, London, SE1 9BG

Scholastic LTD, Unit 89E, Lagan Road, Dublin Industrial Estate, Glasnevin, Dublin 11

ISBN 978-1-338-89307-6

10 9 8 7 6 5 4 3   24 25 26 27

Printed in China 62

First printing 2023

Supplementary imagery © Shutterstock

AMAZING15, Project Management and Design • **JOANNA FARROW**, Writer and Food Styling
KATE LLOYD, Additional Writing and Copy Editing • **LIZ & MAX HAARALA HAMILTON**, Photography
DOMINIQUE ELOÏSE ALEXANDER, Prop Styling • **REBECCA WOODS**, Food Styling

Thank you to our models:
Ausra, Coco, Farrah, Max, Thomas

Special thanks to:
Alysia Scudamore at Urban Angels, Grace Oxenham for props assistance, Lara York Designs

SAMANTHA SWANK, Editor, Scholastic • **SALENA MAHINA**, Designer, Scholastic
VICTORIA SELOVER, Director - Editorial Publishing, Warner Bros. Discovery
KATIE CAMPBELL, Senior Design Manager – Global Publishing, Warner Bros. Discovery
LUKE BARNARD, Product Development Manager – The Blair Partnership